ch

THE
ARTIFACT
HUNTER'S
HANDBOOK

THE ARTIFACT HUNTER'S HANDBOOK

Michael Hudoba

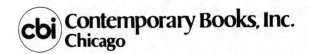 Contemporary Books, Inc.
Chicago

Library of Congress Cataloging in Publication Data

Hudoba, Michael.
  Artifact hunter's handbook.

  "State-by-state listing of archaeologists and
publications": p.
  Includes index.
  1. Archaeology—Handbooks, manuals, etc.
2. Antiquities—Collection and preservation—Handbooks,
manuals, ect.   3. Archaeology—United States—
Societies, etc.—Directories.   I. Title.
CC75.5.H8   1978   930'.1'028   78-23686
ISBN 0-8092-7641-0
ISBN 0-8092-7640-2 pbk.

Published by Contemporary Books, Inc.
180 North Michigan Avenue, Chicago, Illinois 60601
Manufactured in the United States of America
Library of Congress Catalog Card Number: 78-23686
International Standard Book Number: 0-8092-7641-0 (cloth)
                                    0-8092-7640-2 (paper)

Published simultaneously in Canada by
Beaverbooks
953 Dillingham Road
Pickering, Ontario L1W 1Z7
Canada

Contents

Introduction

IF YOU'VE EVER casually reached your hand down to feel between the cushions of a sofa or automobile seat or glanced down into the street at curb side while waiting for the light to change, you already possess some of the mystique that motivates the artifact hunter. The artifact hunter hopes not so much to find something of monetary value as to find something unexpected—a small surprise to interrupt the routine of an otherwise ordinary day.

An artifact, simply put, is an object made or modified by human hands. An artifact is a palpable link to the exciting story of a civilization's past—its culture, its art, its aspirations, and its failures. Through artifacts you can trace the history of a civilization with clues to how its people lived from day to day and coped with their surroundings in their struggles for food, clothing, and shelter. Students and scholars have reconstructed civilizations long since vanished from the face of the earth using artifacts as evidence.

Not every artifact hunter will find a treasure such as the Rosetta stone, the key to ancient Egypt's alphabet. It provided scholars with the means to translate the hieroglyphics that told of the glories of a six-thousand-year-old civilization. But who knows what you may come up with? Artifacts can be found everywhere. A Bedouin peasant's curiosity about a cave, for example, led to the discovery of the Dead Sea Scrolls, hidden for thousands of years. It almost seems sacrilegious to call the scrolls artifacts, in view of their immeasurable contribution to the knowledge of the Old Testament, but artifacts they are. Man fashioned the writing implements, processed the materials on which the scrolls were written, and devised the holders and storage containers that preserved them through the years. The fact that the scrolls were discovered after thousands of years by a typical individual should tell you something. Wherever man has set foot on the earth—literally since the dawn of civilization—it is likely that he left behind some evidence of his presence. And as the discovery of the scrolls illustrates, finding artifacts is not limited to archaeologists or historians.

Are you the least bit curious about your surroundings? Do you recall the history lessons you learned in school? Do you observe the natural phenomena of your environment? You have the makings of an artifact hunter. Add to that deductive logic and an interest in healthful recreation, and you can round out the profile of an artifact hunter. Above all, include a touch of patience. Not every field trip or excursion is guaranteed to produce results. Were it so, success would become routine and the pleasure of the unexpected would pale into the commonplace.

This book is written for the American artifact hunter. It will provide clues on where to look for artifacts, what precisely to look for, and how. Each chapter will describe a period of history—for example, the colonial period or the westward expansion—and tell what artifacts are likely to be found from that period and in what locations.

The American artifact hunter is in a unique position— artifacts from Indian civilizations that flourished before Columbus' discovery of the continent are still being discovered with amazing frequency. Challenging questions remain to be answered through the discovery of artifacts. For example, some evidence has been turned up to indicate that the Vikings settled on the coast of the continent centuries before 1492, and speculation remains about possible early explorations by the Celts and the Egyptians.

Some artifact hunters dive for Spanish treasure ships off the coast of Florida. A friend of the author found and traced the anchor of the famous mutinied ship *Bounty*. Many artifacts from the colonists and pioneers still await the sharp eye of an artifact hunter.

Whether it be a crudely fashioned stone tool of prehistoric man, a finely made American Indian arrowhead, a pottery piece from a colonist's cabin kitchen, a hand-crafted pioneer tool, or any of the thousands of items used and discarded by our forebears, such artifacts carry with them an intriguing challenge—to trace our country's past through the objects discarded by its earliest residents.

Artifacts are not difficult to find, if you know where to look. As a matter of fact, sometimes you don't even have to know where to look; you may stumble upon an accidental find. Indian arrowheads, for example, are commonly found in farmers' fields, and such chance discoveries often set the finder on a lifelong pastime of hunting for artifacts.

You can find artifacts in your own back yard, on a camping or fishing trip, or on a carefully planned excursion into the countryside. Included in the chapters that follow will be tips on prime artifact hunting locations such as:

River banks and bluffs. Look for quartz and flint chips, arrowheads, and piles of discarded mussel shells for evidence of Indian encampments. Check where floodwater has gouged into the bank.

Country dirt roads. Check where a road runs near a river or where the road builder has gouged into the hillside.

Caves. Used as shelter and a source of flint for tools by the Indians.

Farmers' fields, especially those bordering streams or rivers.

Look after a rain, which will expose partially buried stones and wash clean quartz and flint. Good spots also for battlefield relics.

Excavations of any kind. Wherever the earth is disturbed, long buried items may turn up.

Urban renewal areas. Good places to salvage architectural details such as fireplace mantels, doors, decorative moldings, and iron work.

Along water or land trails used by the voyageurs, cattlemen, and pioneers. Look especially for likely campsites, for example, near the rapids on riverbanks.

Someone once said, "Yesterday's trash is today's treasure." That's what artifacts are all about.

Happy hunting!

THE
ARTIFACT
HUNTER'S
HANDBOOK

1

A Touch of
Archaeology

THE ARTIFACT HUNTER, whatever his or her degree of interest, is a practitioner in one of the more absorbing scientific disciplines—archaeology. Archaeology is the science of deducing man's history from the relics of his past. The relics—or artifacts—are tangible and visible records of how man lived before he learned the art of written history.

The word *archaeology* may suggest to you a picture of individuals bedecked in pith helmets, busily digging and sifting the hot sands of the Near East, seeking bones and pottery fragments among the ruins of long-forgotten cities. But archaeology is not limited to the study of pre-Christian, Greek, Roman, or Persian civilizations which ceased to flourish many thousands of years ago. Our Western Hemisphere has yielded already a wealth of ancient materials to the explorations of archaeologists and artifact hunters, and the pre-Columbian civilizations of the Incas, Mayas, and Aztecs of Central and South America pose as yet unanswered questions to students of man's development.

One issue that continues to challenge archaeologists is the emergence of man on the North American continent. Scientists concur that in ancient times a bridge of land across the Bering Strait linked the continents of Asia and America and that the ancestors of the Indians found their way to the Western Hemisphere across that bridge from northeast Asia. Campsites dating back fifteen to twenty-five thousand years that have been excavated by archaeologists add support to this theory, but more evidence is needed to fill in the details.

As the migration spread across the length and breadth of the hemisphere, cultures began to emerge, following the patterns of cultural development in the Old World. The opportunities for discovery of clues about the migration and cultural development are almost unlimited. In the past five years, for example, artifact hunters in Virginia have turned up relics which led to the discovery of the site of an Indian civilization that predates some of the settlements excavated on the shores of the Mediterranean. Using the clues turned up by artifact hunters, archaeologists and graduate students are digging and sifting the earth at the site of the Indian encampment, estimated to be more than ten thousand years old and located less than a hundred miles from Washington, D.C., a population center of more than three million.

A how-to handbook on artifact hunting can only skim lightly over a subject so broad as archaeology, which covers the story of man since he first emerged as a being capable of using brain power to cope with the forces of environment.

Man emerged in the Stone Age as a being whose existence and subsistence were devoted to gathering wild fruits, nuts, and berries; fishing; and hunting wild animals. From the use of pointed sticks as spears, he gradually began to adopt the native materials of stone, flint, shell, bone, and antler to fashion the first primitive tools. These were formed as simple tools with a single sharpened edge. Artifacts of these durable materials are found on all the continents and generally follow the same pattern of development.

Tool development progressed from the single-edged pebble

tools to bifacial, or two-edged, tools to flake tools and finally to blade tools. Over the ages, specialized tools were developed, including weapons.

Since quartz is a common native material found all over the world and is noted for its hardness and suitability for cleavage into sharp, shell-like surface edges, it is not surprising that early man discovered its capabilities and used it to fashion flake and blade tools. Most of the early artifacts found in the United States are made of flint, a rock of the quartz family.

Alibates flint, from the Alibates flint quarries in Texas. *(Photo by Fred. E. Mang, Jr., National Park Service, U.S. Department of the Interior)*

Were it not for man's early belief in a physical existence after death, many of the artifacts of his emerging years would still be undiscovered. The tools, weapons, and possessions of early man were buried in the graves with him for use in the next world.

Such grave sites, as repositories of artifacts, have proven to be invaluable sources for the work and study of archaeologists. They also are a bonanza for artifact hunters. Classic examples of such grave sites are the Indian mounds found in Georgia and Ohio, where careful excavations have been made under the supervision of archaeologists.

How the transition from stone to bronze tools came about remains a subject for conjecture. Copper and iron commonly occur in nature together, and so perhaps man discovered their malleability by accident. You may picture an early man keeping a blazing fire alive to ward off the cold and wild animals. Fire making was difficult, and so fires were nurtured over long periods of time. Such a fire, located above a deposit of copper, may have served as a primitive furnace, eventually converting the ore into metal.

From the ashes of such fire pits, which also yielded sharp-edged pieces of fractured quartz, primitive man must have curiously plucked hard-edged metal lumps. His attempts to sharpen the edges would have revealed the workability of the rough metal form. It is only a guess. But surely the desperate struggle to survive in a hostile environment forced man constantly to seek improvement of his primitive tools.

Bronze, and eventually iron, became common materials. The artifacts of these periods reveal an increased sophistication in the development of tools, utensils, weapons, ornaments, and coins.

Sometime in this early period of progress in the use of bronze and iron, communication and trade among neighboring tribes must have developed. Again, you may visualize the ingenious early man who recognized the value of his source of copper. Instead of pursuing the rigors and uncertainty of a dangerous hunt to procure food, he learned that he could trade the ore or roughly fashioned tools for food. Somewhere after such a beginning, tokens as primitive coins began to emerge to facilitate such trade.

The artifacts found at sites in the United States support the theory that trade was carried on among tribes. Artifacts which do not belong to a particular culture and which are traceable to a distant location have been found at excavation sites, reinforcing the notion of tribal exchanges.

The colonists, when they arrived, established trade with Indians. The white man's artifacts sometimes are found among the remains of Indian villages.

Your fascination with artifact hunting will lead you inevitably to curiosity about the people who fashioned or made the artifacts. You may find yourself on the threshold of the study of archaeology, which in turn can enhance your interest and make you a better informed artifact hunter.

As an amateur artifact hunter, you should seek to learn some basic information about archaeology and history. Each continent has an archaeological history, detailing man's progression from prehistoric times through the Stone Age, Bronze Age, and Iron Age. The environment and climate of each particular area influence man's ascent from a primitive state to civilization. Archaeologists, patiently uncovering ancient habitations from each period of man's existence, have contributed raw materials for study. Using the raw materials as evidence, they have produced a logical scenario of the history of man.

You can explore the subject of archaeology in a number of places in most metropolitan areas. The library should be your first stop. Most libraries contain at least a shelf of books devoted to archaeology and the early history of man, and the librarian can provide more extensive references on the subject.

If you are lucky enough to live near a natural history museum, you can study carefully preserved and cataloged exhibits of artifacts that may well reflect the archaeological history of the area in which you live. Familiarize yourself with the nature of the objects of your searches. How do they look and feel? Imagine how they may have looked buried in the mud at the bottom of a stream bed or caked with soil from a farmer's field. Knowing the appearance of the artifacts that have been found in your area will help make your hunt successful.

Interview the curator of the museum, if possible. He or she may be able to give you firsthand details about some of the more exciting discoveries or provide you with the names of people who live in your city who actively study and hunt for artifacts.

Attend meetings of an archaeology, antiquities, or history society in your town, or get in touch with the state archaeological society. Addresses of such organizations and the publications they produce are provided at the end of this book. Such groups may have accumulated a body of information on the archaeology of your region, and it may be available to you in published form. Check your state university or a college in your vicinity for information. You may be able to get permission to use its library, or you may be able to talk with a professor of archaeology who has worked in the area.

Whether you intend to delve deeply into the subject of artifact hunting or simply to pursue your hobby casually, contact with others who share your interest is certainly helpful and fun. You'll be struck by the importance of such contact when you make a discovery or find an artifact that you know nothing about. You'll need to share your find with an expert who can provide you with more detailed information. Should your find prove to be a clue to a potentially significant archaeological discovery, consultation with an archaeologist is crucial. Your discovery could lead to a major contribution to the knowledge of man's early presence in your community.

Remember that haphazard digging at an archaeological site could cause a tragedy. Such unsupervised disturbance at the site of an ancient home of man has taken place enough times to leave gaps of information in archaeological history all over the world.

2

Artifact Hunting Restrictions

THE SIGNIFICANCE of Stone Age artifacts was not understood or appreciated until the eighteenth century. If artifacts were noticed at all during the Dark Ages, such primitive tools were dismissed as objects belonging to witches and dwarfs. Archaeology had not emerged yet as a science, and the great national museums in Europe had not yet been developed. Whenever excavations were made, the sculpture, pottery, coins, and jewelry fell into the hands of private collectors.

Gravesites marked by surface structures or exposed by the elements, along with tombs from the Bronze Age, were desecrated for the treasures they contained. Such careless and wanton vandalism did irreparable damage and has left gaps in subsequent efforts to study and learn the details of the history of man. It has not made the work of archaeologists easier. It was almost inevitable, because of the high degree of civilization achieved by the Egyptians, Greeks, Romans, and Biblical cultures and the high quality of their artifacts, that the remains of their civilizations would become the principal targets of such vandalism.

The Western Hemisphere was not immune to such destruction either. Spanish conquistadors raided the highly civilized Incas, Mayas, and Aztecs to gather gold and art objects made of gold. Ironically, Caribbean hurricanes and the hazards of uncharted waters wrecked many heavily laden Spanish treasure ships, almost as if by vengeance. While treasure hunters have located and salvaged many such wrecks on the ocean bottom, many more still await discovery in the waters of the Spanish main, off South and Central America, and the Florida coast.

The development of archaeology as a science heightened the appreciation of historic sites of ancient civilizations, and as a result governments have imposed limitations and restrictions on archaeological exploration and excavation. Government permission now is required to conduct such projects in many locations, and supervision of the finding of artifacts is strictly enforced, treating them as national treasures. Should you wish to negotiate for permission to conduct archaeological exploration in a foreign country, write or call the country's embassy in Washington, D.C.

Restrictions also are imposed in the Western Hemisphere, where there is an embargo on the export of artifacts of the pre-Columbian era of the Inca, Maya, Aztec, and Mexican cultures. Florida exercises control over exploration for Spanish treasure ships off its coast, and it demands a share in the proceeds of any recovery. However, the artifact hunter may hope to find Spanish doubloons and pieces of eight on the beaches of Florida and the Keys.

The U.S. Forest Service has imposed restrictions on unauthorized digging and on the taking of Indian artifacts on national forest lands. This also applies specifically to national forests located in North Carolina, Kentucky, Tennessee, and Virginia, where a cultural resource specialist monitors the regulation. You should check with the supervisor of a national forest in the area in which you wish to conduct an artifact hunt, and you should familiarize yourself with the regulations that apply. Usually, the only way you can get permission to participate in an archaeological exploration on national forest land is to be a member of a team working with an approved permit under the direction of a professional archaeologist.

The major sites of Indian civilization have been declared national historic sites. Certain states also have reserved historic sites, including Indian mounds and archaeological sites. Strict regulations apply to activities in both state and national sites.

The National Park Service, which administers some thirty million acres of national parks, monuments, battlefield, and historic sites, including the ancient Indian pueblos, enforces strict prohibition against disturbing the flora, fauna, and land in any way. Frustrated with the swarms of battlefield memento hunters wantonly digging and scarring the landscape of the battlefield sites, the park service seeded thousands of metal discs into the fields in Fredericksburg and Spotsylvania, Virginia. The discs are designed to confuse the metal detectors used by artifact hunters to search for war relics.

Such restrictions are necessary, but should not discourage you in your pursuit of artifact hunting. Remember that national and state historic sites have been preserved as national treasures and are established for the use and enjoyment of all. Although it might appear as though there are no remaining spots for you to follow your hobby, keep in mind that the total of national park and national forest land is only a small fraction of the two billion surface acres of land in the United States. Park lands are open to the public for walking, hiking, and enjoyment. Should you discover clues that indicate an undiscovered site of potential archaeological significance, you may attempt, through official channels, to develop a program for exploration.

Corporations also hold huge tracts of land, principally as forest reserve for timber production and mineral leases. Most such companies have a liberal policy for public access to such areas; the main reservation is the matter of corporate liability for injury or damage. A company prefers to know who is on its land, particularly if there is to be any exploratory digging, and it is important for you to get in touch with the local representative of the corporation for permission to conduct such activity.

Most land, however, is privately owned, and trespass laws apply. Private landowners take pride in their holdings, and they are likely to take a dim view of a stranger found digging or prowling around their farms. If you first obtain permission from the owner to dig on the land, you not only will avoid embarrassment or possible prosecution for trespassing, but you also might establish a relationship that could be an asset to your exploration. The landowner, particularly if the farm has been in the same family for generations, might be able to tell you some of the history of the immediate area and possibly provide clues that would be helpful for an artifact hunting exploration.

Let me relate a personal experience to illustrate the point. I own a farm with a house that dates back to the pre-Revolutionary period of colonial history. When two strangers drove up to the door one day and asked permission to do some research on the farm, I was a bit apprehensive. My fears were dispelled immediately. They explained they were Civil War buffs, and their research indicated that a skirmish had taken place somewhere near the site of my farm. From historical records, they had plotted the movement of small detachments of infantry and pieced together an account of the encounter. They had traced and followed the course of the movement, and with a metal detector had already located shell fragments and a musket. From the historical account, especially from the physical description of the terrain and mountain peaks, their charts indicated that the site of the fighting was in the area of my farm.

I was fascinated enough to give permission, and they promised to give me a report of their findings. They returned at the end of the day to say that they had concluded that the action was to the west on a neighboring farm. Although this was a disappointment to me, my conversation with them provided me with much information about the Civil War movement in the area that would otherwise have taken me considerable time to develop.

Had I discovered them prowling around the farm, it is most likely that the confrontation would have been antagonistic. They would not have been able to complete their study, and I would have been deprived of the interesting history about the area surrounding my farm.

Much of your artifact hunting will be conducted on private land. The key is the landowner. It doesn't take much extra time to get prior permission, and doing so is not only essential but may also produce an unexpected source of information.

This chapter on restrictions is not written to discourage you as an artifact hunter; it is designed to help you avoid unpleasant and unnecessary episodes. With the population expanding as it is, the amount of wild, unattended, or unsupervised land has been reduced. To be a successful artifact hunter, you must learn to deal with landowners, whether governmental, corporate, or private. If you are aware of this and if you approach the person who controls the land for permission, you may reap unexpected dividends.

3

Artifacts—What They Are

ARTIFACTS ARE FOUND all over the world, but this book is limited to those which have been found in the Western Hemisphere, especially in the United States, and to the types which you may hope to discover yourself.

Stone Age artifacts are the rarest and most prized specimens. Primitive and aboriginal man was many thousands of years away from the Bronze and Iron ages, and his tools for hunting and primitive agriculture were fashioned from readily available native materials such as stone, bone, shell, antler, and horn.

He led a solitary life, with a small family cluster wandering in search of and following the movements of wild animals. They sought shelter in caves, which are today among the most likely places in which to discover the traces of his existence. The earliest tools were pointed sticks and clubs, most of which have long since rotted away, leaving such durable materials as stone, horn, bone, and shell, which may have formed spear points or ax heads. There are exceptions. For example, a primitive man who became trapped in a peat bog or quicksand may have dropped his wooden tools and they may have been preserved over time.

You need a practiced eye to discover crudely fashioned, single-edged stone implements. These tools, used for killing game, consisted principally of spear points, ax heads, and knife-like edges for cutting. The methods used by primitive people to fashion such tools were similar all over the world. They included percussion chipping, pressure chipping, pecking, grinding, and carving. The materials used for projectile points, axes, and cutting tools were, according to their native availability, quartz and siliceous rocks such as flint, chert, and jasper. Implements for food grinding, usually shaped by pecking with a sharp rock, were made from coarse-grained rocks such as limestone, sandstone, granite, or basalt, whatever was convenient to the tool-making site. Objects to be carved or polished were made from similar rocks or from fine-grained materials. Because of its brittleness, obsidian, a volcanic, glass-like rock, did not come into use until chipping techniques had advanced to a high level of skill.

Flint was quite common and was widely used for tools by the Indians. When cracked, flint breaks with a shell-like fracture into a sharp, jagged cutting edge. These edges were worked into the desired shape by striking with a chipping action or by a pressure method, using a flint edge, antler, or bone to flake off the cleavages to the required sharpness. Wherever an Indian toolmaker once camped, the by-products of chips and flakes remain as clues for the artifact hunter.

Pebble tools were made by breaking smooth stream pebbles, then chipping the broken end by the percussion method into a cutting edge. The unbroken rounded end conveniently fits into the palm for use.

American Indians refined and developed the Stone Age pebble, bifacial, and hand-ax tools. They developed specialized tools, including arrowheads, spears, tomahawks, axes, skinning stones, knives, and bone fishhooks. They fashioned stone mortars and pestles for grinding corn, pottery for storing food and cooking, stone pipes, and ornaments. The Indians made core tools or fist

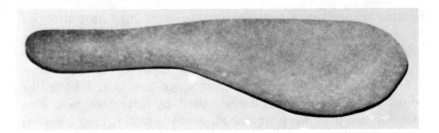

Indian hammer discovered by Michael Hudoba. *(Photo by Michael Hudoba)*

axes from stream pebbles or from very large flakes of flint. They fashioned the tools on both faces by percussion chipping.

Knives were formed from large flakes. They were well shaped and thinned by percussion chipping and often refined by pressure flaking. In New York State and the Northeast, the Indians used slate for knives.

Indian scrapers occur in many shapes—oval, circular, turtle-back, or thumbnail—depending on the original size of the base material. One side of a smooth face was left unworked, while the opposite face was shaped by percussion and finished for its desired use by pressure chipping.

The Indians fastened projectile points to their spears or javelins, the most common and easily recognized of which are the familiar arrowheads. The well-known, fine-shaped, small, sharp tips were used for killing, and the heavier, rough points were used for stunning game.

Food grinding implements were developed as one of the emerging skills of agriculture. The earliest agricultural tool was a slab with a depression gouged in the center to hold maize or corn while it was pounded with a stone hammer. I have in my collection a stone hammer fashioned ingeniously from stream rock. It is about a foot long with a rounded bulbous end that serves as a hammerhead and a handle that nicely fits the hand. Mortars and pestles, along with stone bowls, followed as a sophisticated development. The Indians used flint extensively for their tools. This rock, of the quartz family, is gray, brown, black, or smoky white in appearance. In volcanic regions tools were

Stone tools used by Indians as rolling pins. *(Photo by Kenneth Trobaugh).*

made from obsidian, a glassy volcanic rock usually colored black. These tools are highly prized and common enough to encourage the artifact hunter.

A variety of other artifacts were fashioned or modified by Indians for special functions, including stone fishhooks, awls, sewing needles, points for drilling, chipping tools, and ornaments of shell, mica, copper, silver, and occasionally gold.

It is rare to find an unbroken example of pottery. Basketry, weaving, and leather crafts, because of their nondurable materials, also are rare and are most likely to be found in the arid Southwest.

With the discovery of America and the settlement of the United States, the colonists brought tools and supplies from the Old World, and also designed and fashioned tools and equipment with which to meet the challenges of life in the New World. Colonial relics expand the potential for the artifact hunter.

The colonists, frontiersmen, and their successors, the pioneers, moving to settle the West, were largely self-sufficient. They made most of their own tools and implements. It is possible to trace many items in everyday use today to the ingenuity of our forebears. Here is a potential specialty for the artifact hunter— tracing the development of modern objects back progressively to their early origins. For example, one artifact hunter specializes in collecting axes. As a result of his collecting, his interest in the development of the ax became so absorbing that his collection now is recognized internationally for its completeness in tracing the history of the ax from its prehistoric origins.

Another almost unlimited field for the artifact hunter has opened up with the growth of interest in nineteenth-century nostalgia. Perhaps it is because of our disenchantment with the sameness of machine-made items produced for our daily use that there is such keen interest in handmade artifacts from the not too distant past, particularly items that reflect the individuality of the producer.

The variety of items made by man, used, and discarded over the years is so extensive that it would take volumes even to list them in their numerous categories. You can safely assume that there are collectors specializing in each of these categories. If you have not decided yet on an area of specialization, you may assume that whenever or whatever you choose to collect, you will find company and organized groups to share your interest.

4

Hunting Indian Artifacts

HOW MANY TIMES has a farm boy, walking through a plowed field after a rain, found an arrowhead? How many hunters and fishermen avidly pursuing their sport have found an Indian relic and added artifact hunting to their recreational interests? Indian artifacts can be and have been found in every state of the United States. Your chance of finding an arrowhead, for example, is very good. And such a find is often enough to spark a permanent interest in artifact hunting.

The first artifact evidence of the presence of Indians in the United States dates back some twenty-five thousand years. The durability of the stone tools, plus the accumulation of thousands of years of Indian life across the United States, explain the quantity of artifacts that have been gathered for museum and private collections. In addition, vast numbers of artifacts still lie buried or hidden, awaiting the keen eye of the hunter.

Records indicate that in the Western Hemisphere there were more than four hundred major tribal groups speaking some 160 different languages. There is no way to measure accurately their numbers, but estimates of the total Indian population of the hemisphere around 1200 A.D. have been as high as fifty to seventy-five million. More conservative estimates later scaled this figure down to twenty-five million, and a still more recent estimate settles on five million Indians for the North American continent.

Using even the most conservative estimate of five million Indians, who led in most cases a nomadic existence across the face of America, it is not surprising that their artifacts can be found all over the United States and in provinces of Canada.

The most successful Indian artifact hunters I know are Mr. and Mrs. Edward H. Stokes of Front Royal, Virginia. Their collection, amassed over the years, totals more than six thousand items, is the envy of museums, and provides a mecca for archaeologists and students of Indian archaeology. It was their personal collecting of artifacts in the vicinity of the Shenandoah River that provided clues to the recent discovery of one of the oldest and most significant Indian habitation sites east of the Mississippi River.

Representative Indian tool artifacts, found on surface by Mr. and Mrs. E. H. Stokes. They did no excavating. *(Photos by Kenneth Trobaugh)*

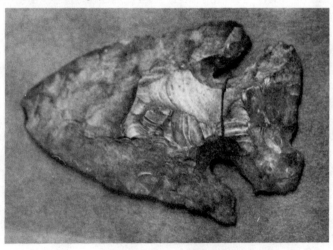

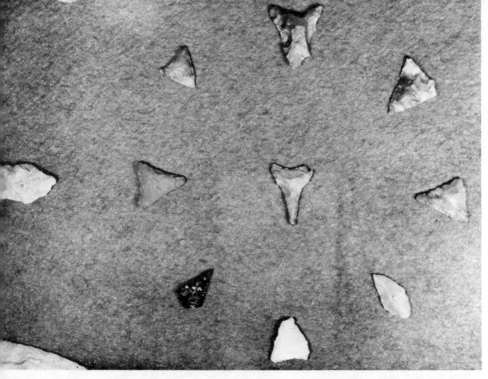

This site now is being explored; diggings begun by professionals about five years ago are well under way, with exciting discoveries being made almost daily during the summer season. These findings will provide a substantial contribution to learning even more about Indians who lived in that area some eleven thousand years ago.

The Thunderbird Museum, located about seven miles south of Front Royal on State Route 340, contains examples taken from this dig. These artifacts are made of brown jasper, a native rock of the quartz family. The deposits of jasper outcroppings helped attract the ancient tribe to the location centuries ago. Here on the site of the diggings, the artifact hunter may come to observe professional archaeologists conducting their excavations and research. Admission proceeds help finance the work.

Mr. and Mrs. Stokes, as amateur artifact hunters, did not do any digging themselves. Their entire collection has been accumulated over many years by collecting artifacts exposed on the surface. Most of their finds were made on fields which had been plowed and tilled, with the most productive time to explore being after a rainstorm.

The Stokeses walk over a field in a regular pattern, attempting to cover the entire area, looking for any objects that the erosive action of the rain may have exposed. The only tools used in their collecting excursions are a sharpened stick, which Mrs. Stokes prefers, and a modified cultivating hoe, which Mr. Stokes swears by. With these simple aids, they probe and turn over the stones and objects which their practiced eyes detect as being different enough to suggest they may have been worked on by human hands.

The artifacts in their collection provide them with memories of many pleasant, healthful, and exciting days of exploration. One of their prizes is a perfectly formed and well-worn stone rolling pin about eighteen inches long. The only other one of its kind that they know about is in the Smithsonian Institution. Another artifact they point to with pride is a fluted flint fishhook, broken in two at the center. The Stokeses found the upper half first, and it remained in their collection for some

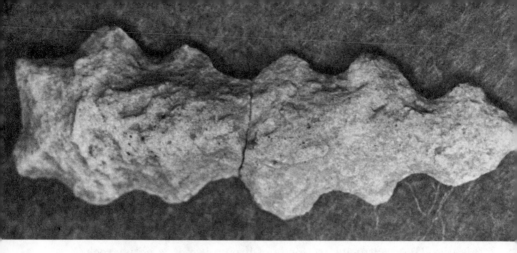

One half of this artifact, a flint-fluted fishhook, was found by the E.H. Stokes couple. Some time later, while surface hunting in the same area, they discovered the missing half. *(Photo by Kenneth Trobaugh)*

time. Mrs. Stokes could not describe the excitement she felt when several years later she found another half of a quartz fishhook and, matching it to the half already in their collection, found it to be the missing portion. The perfectly fitted whole artifact, about two and one-half inches long, is an excellent example of this rare fishing tool.

My own collection of Indian artifacts, extremely modest compared to the Stokes' collection, contains an item I treasure. It is a skinning stone, found years ago while on a hunting trip. The well-worn stone has a sharp edge on the left side evidencing long use and a notch on the right-hand side that fits the thumb of my left hand. I am left-handed, and the perfect fit of the stone has

Indian skinning stone found by the author. *(Photo by Michael Hudoba)*

given me many hours of conjecture over the left-handed Indian who owned it originally. From the worn nature of the stone, I know that he must have been a highly skilled and successful hunter. Who knows how many times he may have saved his people from starvation? What stories he could have told to his soul mate in the twentieth century!

The Indians were basically a nomadic people, particularly the Woodland tribes of the East and the Plains tribes of the Midwest. Surviving by hunting, these tribes were forced to follow the grazing and feeding movements of the game. They covered vast areas in search of new supplies.

Water was a basic necessity for both the Indians and for the animals they hunted. Also, streams and rivers generally provided easy routes through hilly or mountainous terrain. So following the course of rivers was natural for the Indians during their migrations. A river also was a confining boundary to the game, which foraged on its banks. And where a river followed a course between steep hillsides, the movement of game was channeled into narrower travel lanes, making hunting easier.

Whenever a productive hunting area was found, the tribe established a camp from which to hunt. Such a campsite was likely to be on well-drained land, conveniently near the river. River bluffs were ideal sites for camps, with the advantage of a sweeping view to locate grazing herds of prairie game and from which to observe the approach of hostile forces. Spots where rivers joined were also choice campsites.

A campsite served as long as food supplies were adequate: game, fish, shellfish, fruit, berries, and nuts. As these diminished, the tribe would move on toward their winter or summer territory, depending upon the season. Wild game, both birds and animals, required the same type of environment. It provided them with water and food—grass land, woods for nuts, and the accompanying undercover of fruit-bearing bushes, shrubs, vines, and trees.

Whenever I fish a stream or river, I look for areas that might have served as campsites. When I hunt, I go to a productive game area that also contains a promising campsite with an outcropping of quartz nearby that might have provided the raw materials for toolmaking. This program has helped me add to my own collection of artifacts. It has been successful often enough for me to continue combining fishing or hunting trips with artifact hunting or discovering localities to which I might return for further exploration.

Indian artifact discovered by the author on fishing trip. *(Photo by Michael Hudoba)*

Whenever an Indian campsite was used for any length of time, as was often the case around a productive food and game producing area, the tribe would return to the same general site year after year. Such an area is most likely to yield artifacts.

There are old campsites along rivers in Kentucky and Tennessee with large mounds of shells accumulated by the Indians using the abundant freshwater mussels. At Indian Knoll on Green River in Kentucky a deep shell heap, 250 feet by 500 feet, marks the site of a long-used camp.

Life at these campsites was centered on the regimen of day-to-day survival. The hunters searched for game, and the youngsters were left behind the gather nuts, fruit, berries, and shellfish. The women prepared food and worked deer, elk, or buffalo hides for sinew and covering. Older tribesmen fashioned tools and projectile points such as arrowheads and spears. All this activity inevitably left telltale debris, such as chips from flaking flint to make the arrowheads, spears, axes, and other tools or the inevitable careless losses that occurred in daily living and in making and breaking camp.

The discovery of a litter of quartz and flint chips, among which is likely to be discarded, partially made arrowheads that fractured poorly, is a certain sign of the presence of Indian activity. It is promising evidence and demands that the artifact hunter make a careful search of the area. Clues such as this are most likely to lead to the discovery of Indian artifacts, suggesting the possibility that you as an artifact hunter have some virgin territory to explore.

Even the chance find of one arrowhead should alert you.

Although the projectile point may represent an arrow that missed its target and was lost in flight, it is evidence that a hunter passed that way. A careful search of the vicinity should be made, bearing in mind the basic essentials of a campsite, for the hunter may not have been too far from his tribal home.

In Virginia, the Shenandoah River, its North and South forks, and the slopes of the Blue Ridge Mountains have yielded generous numbers of artifacts. With its temperate climate, bountiful hardwood and vast forests, and outcroppings of flint and jasper, this area was a favorite hunting and camping site for the Indians who migrated here annually from the north. Many farm boys have found artifacts as they worked their land. It is a fertile area for the artifact hunter to explore.

Another way to develop clues to the artifact potential of an area is to visit the local museum. Antique or souvenir shops also may have arrowheads and Indian artifacts on display for sale. A chat with the owner might uncover some local sources of information on likely exploration sites.

Most state governments employ a staff archaeologist who may be able to provide you with publications on the state's archaeological history. Archaeology or history departments of a state or local university or the public library are also starting points for clues to areas in which to search for artifacts.

The precolonial Indian population, although comparatively small in number, extended over areas in virtually every state. Most of the tribes lived nomadically, but a few developed agriculture as an auxiliary food source. In the Southwest, agriculture reached a high degree of skill; Indians there abandoned nomadic movement to live in central communities of cliff dwellings. In the Northwest, the Indians developed a culture related to water and the plentiful supply of salmon. The life of the Indians of the prairies and plains was influenced by the great herds of buffalo.

Studying the environment and natural resources which substantially influenced a tribe's way of life will enhance your opportunity for success in artifact hunting. Publications on the history of the tribes that lived in your area will provide the information on their habits and life patterns. With some knowledge of their way of life, you may look for the kind of environment that could have supported such a life. Although it may be some trouble, this preliminary research and study will limit the amount of territory to explore and may reduce the number of fruitless field trips and time spent on barren search, making your hobby that much more interesting.

Caves

The Indians used caves as a simple alternative to building shelters. A cave of sufficient size, located near water and plentiful supplies of native fruits and berries, with abundant quantities of game in the vicinity, would be used year after year. The floors of such caves bear accumulations of items from years of use by untidy and careless inhabitants. Residual debris includes discarded tools and projectile points.

There are caves in almost every state, but they occur most frequently in the Appalachian Mountains, stretching from Pennsylvania through Virginia, West Virginia, Maryland, Kentucky and Tennessee into northern Georgia and Alabama; in the Ozarks of Missouri and Arkansas; and in South Carolina, central Georgia, southern Alabama, western Florida, south-central Indiana, north-central California, west Texas, and eastern New Mexico.

Cave exploration, or spelunking, as it is popularly known, requires special equipment and techniques to help ensure maximum safety. A citizens' band radio will link you to the outside world, but it will not prevent accidents. There are dangers that could imperil the unwary and inexperienced, and it is strongly recommended that you obtain expert advice before venturing into this phase of exploration. In areas where caves are prevalent, there is most likely an organization of spelunkers, or an expert speleogist who can advise you on safe exploration techniques.

Nevertheless, caves are a good potential source for the artifact hunter, and exploring them could lead to the discovery of a cache of artifacts. An excellent book with a great amount of useful information about caves and their exploration is *Exploring American Caves* by Franklin Folsom.

The cliff dwellers and Pueblo Indians of the Southwest began using caves sometime between 9000 and 7000 B.C. Hundreds of centuries of life in those caves yielded a wealth of artifacts to enrich our knowledge of ancient habitation. The arid climate of the region contributed to the preservation of ancient artifacts in the dry caves, including those of wood, basketry, and leather not found elsewhere.

Gila Cliff Dwellings, New Mexico.
(Photo by National Park Service, U.S. Department of the Interior)

Who knows what discoveries lie ahead in this specialized type of exploration? A good example is Sandia Cave, located near Folsom, New Mexico. Kenneth Davis, a student at the University of New Mexico, located an opening in the face of a cliff on a weekend exploration trip. The opening led to a tunnel, where Davis gathered a cigar box of pottery fragments. He took them to archaeologist Dr. Frank C. Hibben at the university, who

Long House Ruins, Bandelier National Monument, New Mexico. These cliff ruins are one of the most accessible features of the monument. *(Photo by Fred E. Mang, Jr., National Park Service, U.S. Department of the Interior)*

went to the cave to make a routine check. As he dug deeper into the floor of the cave he uncovered finely wrought tools, with tiny chips removed to make cutting edges and a distinctive groove running down the center of each side. Because of the unique style of the projectile points and the location of their discovery, they were named Folsom points, and the men who used them were called Folsom men. Along with the Folsom points, bones of

Ancient cliff dwellings, part of the Bandelier National Monument, New Mexico. *(Photo by National Park Service, U. S. Department of the Interior)*

Aztec Ruins National Monument, New Mexico. *(Photo by George A. Grant, National Park Service, U.S. Department of the Interior)*

an extinct bison were found. Radiocarbon tests dated them between 9000 and 7000 B.C.

Dr. Hibben explored the cave over the course of four summers, digging deeper and deeper until finally the site yielded even older points. These were more crudely fashioned flaked points with one corner notch. Named Sandia points, they were dated back some thirty thousand years by radiocarbon tests.

When one considers that this discovery was made only within the past few decades along with the find made five years ago in Virginia, both of which contributed significantly to information about the life of ancient man in the United States, the challenge and opportunity for the artifact hunter is obvious. There are thousands of American caves awaiting discovery and exploration.

Caves were also sources of material for stone tools. When flint is first mined, it is worked and shaped easily into points for arrowheads, spears, and cutting tools. In his book *Wyandotte Cave*, George F. Jackson explains that southern Indiana was a rich source of flint and that Indians mined the material extensively for their tools. Many artifacts have been found in southern Indiana, including the working areas where the flint was shaped into tools.

Chaco Canyon National Monument, New Mexico. Note the small semi-subterranean rooms called kivas, used for ceremonial purposes. This large pueblo was built in the late 1000s. *(Photo by National Park Service, U.S. Department of the Interior)*

The artifact hunter who locates a deposit source of flint should look for evidence of Indian presence, either signs of mining activity such as chunks of artificially broken stone, or a working

Aztec ruins, New Mexico. Indian burial artifacts discovered in ruins. *(Photo by George A. Grant, National Park Service, U.S. Department of the Interior)*

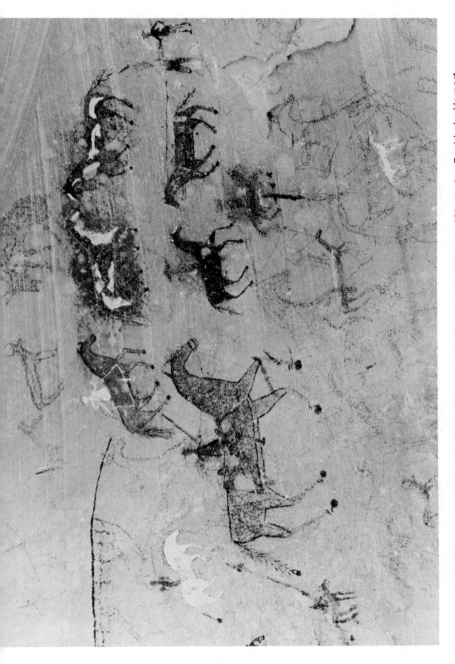

Canyon de Chelly, Arizona. Navajo Indian pictograph in Canyon de Muerto. (Photo by David de Harpart, National Park Service, U.S. Department of the Interior)

area with its telltale chips of flint and partially formed points. It could indicate the probability of finding Indian artifacts in the area. Indians also mined copper in the Great Lakes area and sheets of mica in the Appalachians, minerals, which were used for fashioning ornaments.

I located two workshop areas near flint deposits, one near a spring and the other on a hill overlooking a stream. These contained artifacts of partially made points, discarded because the cleavage was damaged by a careless or faulty move in chipping. I took only a few of the best examples. As far as I know, this site is still my secret, and like a treasured fishing spot it shall remain so until an ingenious, enterprising artifact hunter comes along to share my secret.

The National Park Service administers as national monuments a number of sites devoted to the cliff dwellers and Pueblo Indians. These are the Aztec Ruins, Bandelier, Chaco Canyon, Gila Cliff Dwellings, and Pecos, all in New Mexico, and Mesa Verde in Colorado. One of the best-known examples of a great pueblo is the Taos Pueblo in northern New Mexico. The Pueblos were established there a hundred years before Columbus discovered America and inhabited it for more than six hundred years.

Mound Builders

While the cliff dwellers and Pueblo Indians built lasting evidence of their presence and culture in the Southwest, the drainage basin of the Mississippi River and the Southeast was the scene of another emerging culture which also left unmistakable evidence of inhabitation—the mound builders.

Around 500 B.C. the practice of building burial mounds began to spread, reaching into the eastern and southern United States. The most spectacular example is the Hopewell culture in Hamilton County in southern Ohio, named for the farm where the mounds were first scientifically explored. The Hopewell culture reached into Indiana, Illinois, Wisconsin, Michigan, Iowa, Kansas, Tennessee, Pennsylvania, and New York. Today, the National Park Service administers two areas as national historic sites: the Mound City Group, Ohio, and Effigy Mounds, Iowa.

This culture developed as a farming population which still relied on hunting, fishing, and gathering wild nuts, fruits, seeds, and roots. These Indians built earthworks that served as burial mounds and as bases for religious purposes. The mounds contained artifacts representing the wealth of the deceased. The Hopewell peoples also developed trade, as indicated by materials found in the mounds from as far away as the Rocky Mountains, the Gulf of Mexico, and the Atlantic coast. Artifacts from the Hopewells can also be found in those distant places.

It is interesting to note that one of the earliest diggings conducted in a scientific manner was done by Thomas Jefferson on an Indian mound in Virgina. Jefferson made careful notes and records of his observations during his excavations of the site; he may rightly be called a pioneer in archaeology.

Around 1200 A.D. the Indians of the bottomlands of the Mississippi River, depending more and more on growing maize, began to develop sophisticated cultivation techniques. These people settled into a more sedentary life centered in large villages spread through the south and central Mississippi valley. The people of the Mississippi culture built large pyramidal temple mounds which became the center of their villages. Some of these temples were still being used when the first Spanish explorers arrived. It is interesting to speculate on the sources of their inspiration.

The scale of the public works in the Mississippi culture can be estimated from the largest of the Mississippi earthworks, Monk's Mound near Cahokia, Illinois, which measures 1,000 feet in length, more than 700 feet in width, and is still 100 feet high. Another such example is located at Etowah, near Cartersville, Georgia. Such an indication of Indian presence is a likely exploration territory for artifact hunters.

Underground Artifacts

The ultimate in artifact hunting is done by trained professionals, usually archaeology students under the supervision of archaeologists. The excavation of a habitation site is carried out according to a carefully planned program. It is in fact an exercise in geometry: squares are precisely plotted on the ground, to be opened with corners true as a surveyor's measurement. There is no haphazard digging. Test cuts are made to reveal layers of earth which must be removed to reach the levels containing evidence of human presence. Notes and photographs are made at each step. Later analysis of these details will reveal to the scientist much information on the age and time of the deposits in the dig. How many centuries of sedimentary deposit of soil were accumulated? Were there other civilizations that used the same location? What was the climate in earlier years? A multitude of questions can be answered using the evidence gathered from the excavation. The information will help to reconstruct the history and development of the culture of the peoples who once lived there.

When the archaeologists reach a productive level, they shift to the delicate work of carving away the deposits of earth. Using small trowels, pocket knives or teaspoons, they begin removing the earth, sweeping it onto a dustpan with a paintbrush, sifting through a sieve to locate any flakes that might have been overlooked. Wherever an object is found, the soil is carved away to leave it on an earth pedestal, so that the precise location of each item can be measured. These are put into a bag with notes so that the laboratory later will be able to mark each piece and keep it together with other discoveries of the same level.

Consider the excitement of discoveries such as those of the Folsom points, described earlier. These points were found under dust debris that had accumulated over thousands of years. The careful excavation told the scientists how long the Folsom man had used the cave. Under the layer of Folsom man's habitation, many feet deeper, patient work unearthed an earlier culture, that of the Sandia man, dating thousands of years further back into history.

Archaeologists making a study in Illinois believe there may be more than 900 sites of ancient Indian habitation in that state. One of the most interesting sites at which diggings have been going on for the past seven years is known as the Koster Site, located near Kampsville, Illinois. The public may visit during the summers to observe work in progress at that site. The archaeologists already have reached a depth of 34 feet going through 12 distinct levels of habitation dating back some seven thousand years, and they are still finding artifacts of ancient people.

Where to Look

A good time to hunt is in the spring and fall, when farmers have plowed and disked their fields. Those bordering on a stream or river are especially good sites for hunting. Ask the farmer for permission to hunt; if he hasn't yet sown his seed, he'll most likely consent. Otherwise, you'll have to wait until after harvest. In the fall, after a rainstorm, the stubble roots that remain after the harvest hold the soil together better for walking in the field. The erosive effect of the rain will expose partially buried stones, washing flint and quartz to make its whiteness stand out.

I usually wear rubber boots which reach just below the knee because some of the soil can get pretty sticky. This footwear is also good protection when wading the shallow edges of rivers or streams. The edge of a river bank accumulates sediment which buries any object, but the shallow edges of the river are washed by floodwater, and I have found artifacts in such locations.

There are also several simple tools that can be helpful in your artifact hunting. A walking stick sharpened to a point or tipped with a metal point can save a great deal of stooping and bending. The point is used to turn over stones. A pocket knife or a small trowel, like those used by archaeologists, is a useful tool to gouge out any buried object whose exposed tip shows promise. Out of habit, I look for the familiar white quartz chips and small pieces of quartz rock, turning them over to see whether they have been altered by hand. The same is true for small rocks whose color or shape is slightly inconsistent with the pattern of native stones and rocks. A bag or small shoulder knapsack also will prove useful, if no more than to carry your lunch; but you may also use the knapsack to hold interesting specimens.

It pays to explore a river bank where a rush of floodwater has gouged into or down the bank. In effect, the river will already have done some strata digging for you.

Hunt for artifacts while taking walks on country dirt roads. Look especially where the road runs near a river. Any area where a road builder has made a cut in a hillside should be examined carefully.

A recent important find of an early Indian campsite was made when a road-building bulldozer cut through the bank of a small stream. An artifact hunter picked up some objects and consulted an archaeologist. Subsequent excavation at the site revealed an oval-shaped depression about thirteen feet by eight feet. It contained a circle of blackened and fire-cracked rocks, along with bones which proved to be those of deer and elk. Scattered in the immediate area were projectile points and objects of European manufacture. It was determined this was an Indian hunting camp, and that the Indians had traded with colonists.

Wherever the earth is disturbed, moved, or excavated, it is possible that long-hidden objects, including artifacts, will be uncovered. There is an increase in numbers of homes being built near rivers, lakes, and scenic hillsides in areas that once were wild. The excavations for these homes may serve to uncover hidden artifacts.

Since the passage of the Environmental Protection Act, which requires environmental impact statements on the effects of a major construction project, there is a prior consideration before bulldozers are allowed to tear up the earth. A proposed project planned for an area which has an archaeological history often will call for the services of an archaeologist to make a study of the site. Should there be any indication that the site may have been the scene of an earlier culture, precautions are taken to avoid destroying such a valuable resource or at least to retrieve artifacts of the culture. A person who finds an artifact in the area of a proposed site could perform a real service by alerting the proper authorities.

5

Hunting Colonial Artifacts

FIVE HUNDRED YEARS before Christopher Columbus discovered land off the southern coast of the North American continent, Lief Ericson, a Viking seaman making a voyage from Greenland, landed on a forested shore which he called Vinland. There was no known record of such a voyage or discovery until 1963, when archaeologists uncovered the remains of a Viking settlement on the northern tip of Newfoundland. According to a radiocarbon study, the settlement dated from about 1000 A.D.

It was Columbus's later discovery, however, that encouraged exploratory voyages from the Old World to the Western Hemisphere. The great powers of Europe began sending expeditions to establish claims in the New World. Spain concentrated on the southern area of America, Florida, the gulf coast of Mexico, Central and South America, and lower California, while Portugal established a claim to Brazil in eastern South America. France staked claim to Canada, the Great Lakes, and Mississippi River drainage to the Gulf of Mexico, and England took possession of the Atlantic coast area between the claims of Spain and France. A Portuguese sea captain, Estevan Gomez, serving the king of Spain, explored the coast of North America from Maine to New Jersey. His reports led the Spaniards to conclude that this region was not too valuable, with the result that Spain ignored the greater part of the Atlantic coast.

The object of these explorations was to find an easier sea route to the riches of the Far East. Rich spices were carried laboriously in small quantities by overland routes from India to Europe. Hoping to gain riches from the large cargoes ships could carry, merchants of the European powers formed pools to outfit ships and, with a king's permission obtained by a promise to share the wealth, sent expeditions to seek an ocean route to India.

No thought of any colonization in the New World was made during these early voyages. The adventuresome sea captains probed the estuaries looking for passages. Landings were made to take on fresh water and to hunt for food supplies.

There is very little likelihood of finding artifacts from these early voyages. Whatever possibility may exist depends upon locating the remains of a forgotten shipwreck somewhere in the then-uncharted waters along the coast sailed by the early voyagers. The ships did carry a supply of trade goods to use in the event that they reached India, and if a ship were ever found, its yield would be a treasure of medieval artifacts.

Spain established the earliest settlement, at St. Augustine, Florida, in 1564. The Dutch colonized New York in 1624, and the Swedes settled in Delaware in 1683. All of these settlements eventually were taken over by England. The English founded eleven of the thirteen colonies, which became the original thirteen states carved out of the wilderness along the Atlantic coast.

The first permanent colony was founded in 1607 at Jamestown, Virginia, by Captain John Smith, who thought he had found a passage to India. Later, he explored up Chesapeake Bay. The other colonial settlements were Massachusetts in 1620, New Hampshire in 1623, Maryland in 1634, Connecticut in 1635, Rhode Island in 1636, North Carolina in 1653, New Jersey in

1664, South Carolina in 1670, Pennsylvania in 1682, and Georgia in 1733.

The early settlements depended on supplies brought across the ocean from the Old World. Access to a safe harbor was one of the prime requisites for the settlement sites chosen. The early colonists became more self-sufficient as they cleared land for farming; 90 percent of the colonists were farmers. They built villages inland, but still were dependent on the easier passage of waterways for moving the products of their labors to ships that would trade supplies to them from England. The waters also provided fish and power for turning mill wheels.

The first colonists faced a whole new way of life in the

This painting by Sidney E. King illustrates the importance of accessibility to ships from England for the settlers of Jamestown. The first permanent English settlement in the New World, founded in 1607, Jamestown was the capital of the Virginia colony until 1698. *(Photo by National Park Service, U.S. Department of the Interior)*

wilderness of the New World. They were forced by necessity to adapt the ways of their old life in Europe to strange new conditions and to develop and fashion tools quickly to reach a state of self-sufficiency. The Swedes of Delaware, for example, introduced the log cabin as the first practical wilderness home. The native Indians, who were well established along the entire Atlantic coast, taught the colonists how to raise new crops. They showed them which fish and wild plants to eat and how to track game.

A scientific archaeological excavation at Jamestown, Virginia, America's oldest English colony. *(Photo by National Park Service, U.S. Department of the Interior)*

As the colonists prospered they produced increasing quantities of products such as tobacco, cotton, rice, furs, and timber. Demand for these commodities grew in England and Europe and the quantity and quality of trade goods brought from the Old World increased. Artifacts of this early colonial period are predominantly English and European in origin.

As the value of colonial goods increased, English ships began to bring in products from India and the Far East—tea and spices and high quality trade goods. The arrival of a ship was a big event to the colonists, and the docks became an important center of community life.

(Above) An illustration of an archaeological excavation at Jamestown. This was an ice pit from the latter seventeenth century. (Below) Also found at Jamestown, portions of barrels, such as this one found at the bottom of a shallow well. *(Photos by National Park Service, U.S. Department of the Interior)*

MANUAL LABOR

wood rasp

crosscut saw

hatchet

hoe

metal edge for wooden shovel blade

In the first years, everyone had to work with his hands. Later, indentured servants contracted to work for a period of years for payment of their passage, board and keep. Still later there were Negro slaves.

These are some of the tools used.

blade and lock wedge plate for plane

auger

wood chisels

hammers

draw knife

Early colonial artifacts of the tools colonists used for their labor in the New World. *(Photo by Ralph H. Anderson, National Park Service, U.S. Department of the Interior.)*

Many of these items were made in England. *(Photo by National Park Service, U.S. Department of the Interior)*

The tobacco-growing plantations of Maryland and Virginia surrounding Chesapeake Bay had their own plantation docks. You can still see remnants of the piles of these old docks as you cruise the bay. Who knows what may lie hidden in the waters surrounding these ruins?

About the time of the Revolution, tensions were building

Conjectural painting by Sidney King, Colonial National Historical Park, Jamestown. Tobacco was a vital export crop for the colonists of the South. *(Photo by National Park Service, U.S. Department of the Interior)*

against the English crown, and Chesapeake Bay became a haven for privateers who captured English trading vessels and plundered upriver plantations. Using shallow-draft boats and an intimate knowledge of bay waters, the privateers could escape pursuit in the shallows of backwater creeks and rivers. Many vessels were sunk or abandoned in such pursuits, and cargoes may still be awaiting discovery by some fortunate artifact hunter.

The flow of trade brought not only essential staples but also fine furniture, silverware, dishes, and other luxury goods, representing the best of the arts and crafts of the Old World artisans. These became family treasures for the colonists.

The colonists themselves had developed skills in producing tools and items for everyday life. These arts and crafts skills grew into the production of prized items of colonial furniture, American pewterware, and a wide assortment of artistically made accessories. Silversmithing flourished, brought to a state of high art by craftsmen such as Paul Revere. Glass makers created choice items of exquisite beauty.

Colonial Williamsburg served as the capital of the Virginia colony. It has been superbly restored: homes, streets, and shops re-create the life and times of colonial Virginia. Here you can

Sgraffito, or "scratch ware," found at Jamestown. Designs were scratched into the upper layer of pliable clay before the ceramic was baked. *(Photo by National Park Service, U.S. Department of the Interior)*

see craftsmen and artisans, outfitted in authentic colonial dress, using the tools and equipment from pre-Revolutionary times. Williamsburg is well worth a visit. You will have an opportunity to study the items used in colonial life.

Colonial artifacts are highly prized and expensive. Antique dealers and collectors have combed potential sources of these items thoroughly for many years. The only reliable sources of colonial artifacts these days are antique shops and estate auctions. Colonial and early American artifacts also may be found at country or farm sales, usually advertised in rural weekly newspapers. However, it's not unlikely that you may find yourself competing with professional antique dealers.

A new phenomenon is the so-called garage sale. If you have a practiced eye, you may find a real bargain at such a sale. Since the items offered for sale are considered useless or are treated as unwanted junk, they may be underpriced. If you pass a sign advertising a garage sale, it may be worth a few minutes of time to examine the display.

The epitome of colonial artifact hunting is the challenge of finding an answer to the mystery of what happened to the Lost Colony of the outer banks of North Carolina. A small band of settlers was left behind to start a settlement. When the supply ship returned three years later the settlers had vanished, and no trace of them has ever been found.

The same outer banks were the site of a unique form of piracy. The waters off the sand dunes that form the shore were uncharted in colonial times, and the trade route north from the Caribbean was very close to shore. Enterprising and unscrupulous residents would hang a lantern from the neck of a mule and turn the animal loose to wander the shore at night. Passing ships, mistaking the light for a beacon marking safety, would follow the erratic course of the wandering mule and wreck on the shoals offshore. The wrecked ship then would be plundered. The area also was used by pirate ships, and during the Civil War blockade-running ships were sunk there. The treacherous waters are still strewn with rotting wrecks and no doubt with countless artifacts.

North Carolina's Underwater Archaeological Research Unit is carrying on an active, unpublicized program of exploration. Its research led to the location of the Civil War ironclad ship, the *Monitor*, as well as Indian canoes dating back centuries. The unit has also found the remains of various shipwrecks and charted them for future exploration.

Colonial life and trade depended to a large extent on the sailing ships from the Old World. The waters leading into most colonial ports were inadequately charted, and since the vessels were shallow drafted they ventured into waters that contained shoals and treacherous hazards. Shipwrecks inevitably occurred.

The waters now are carefully charted and well marked by navigation aids. It is possible to plot the course that the old sailing ships may have taken to reach the port and analyze possible sites that may be the resting place of a shipwreck. Underwater exploration is a comparatively new discipline enhanced by the development of sophisticated equipment and gear. It offers an almost unlimited opportunity for the artifact hunter who takes the time to learn the art of scuba diving.

Unlike the Indians who roamed the land leaving their artifacts in unexpected places, the colonists stayed in settlements, which grew into villages, cities, and great metropolitan areas.

BUILDING HARDWARE

UNEARTHED AT JAMESTOWN

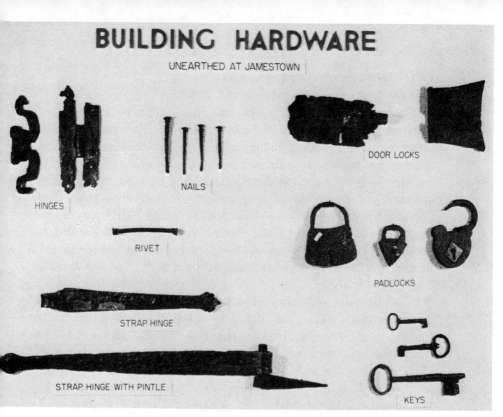

Building hardware unearthed at Jamestown. *(Photo by National Park Service, U.S. Department of the Interior)*

There have been some successful salvage finds in urban renewal areas, particularly of architectural details made by skilled craftsmen—fireplace mantels, doors, decorative moldings, and ironwork. These treasured artifacts are often incorporated into the construction of new homes by appreciative connoisseurs.

Excavation sites for subways and buildings, especially in older parts of cities whose history dates back to colonial times, offer possibilities of discovering interesting artifacts. Homes of the seventeenth and eighteenth century built closely together in the older sections of colonial villages and cities generally had basements with earthen floors. There were no garbage or waste collectors in those days, and people were inclined to throw their trash into the corners of their basements. Bulldozers moving earth and making excavations for urban renewal in the deteriorated sections of older cities dating back to colonial times are likely to uncover such basement dumping areas.

When Dr. and Mrs. William Ray Hepner bought their eighteenth-century house in Baltimore's Fells Point, they found a large hunk of metal in their earth-floored basement, the *Washington Post* reported. It turned out to be the original eighteenth-century iron lock for the front door. They cleaned it, had a new six-inch key made for it, and put it back on their front door. This find inspired a new weekend activity for Baltimore artifact hunters—basement digging. Members of the Archaeological Society of Maryland, who explore old Indian camping grounds around the state, now have added basement digging to their roster of activities.

In addition to old coins, pipe bowls, and fragments of dishes, one basement yielded a number of toy tin horses about two inches high and painted bright red, white, and blue. This basement had been part of a bar used almost continuously since 1790. Innkeepers and bartenders used to sell bowls of tobacco across the bar. After the smoker was finished, he would hand the bowl back to the bartender, who would break off part of the stem. When someone else wanted a smoke, he would refill the bowl. When the stem became too short, the pipe was discarded.

Many homes and farms dating back to the seventeenth and eighteenth centuries still exist in areas of the original colonies surrounding urban areas. If you are fortunate enough to be acquainted with the owner of such a home, you may be able to obtain permission to hunt for artifacts on his or her property.

I own a stone house built in 1740 for Lord Fairfax on his Virginia land grant, which was bought in 1800 by John Marshall, the fourth chief justice of the United States. I have found many artifacts in the house and on the surrounding acreage, including silverware monogrammed with Marshall's "M" and numerous fragments of plates, both imported from Europe and made in the United States. Many of these finds were made while I was tilling the garden and flower beds.

There are traces of old slave quarter cabin foundations and the old kitchen, which was detached from the house. Behind the traces of the kitchen foundation is a gully, that served as a dumping site for broken and discarded dishes and kitchen ware.

Georgian colonial stone house built in 1740, the author's home for the past quarter century. *(Photo by Michael Hudoba)*

Although a metal detector is of little use in searching for Indian artifacts, which are made of flint and stone, it is a valuable tool for the artifact hunter whose interest is discovering artifacts of the colonial or later periods of American life. Most of these items were made of or contain metal, which the detector can locate underground.

Another potential source of colonial artifacts is abandoned colonial home sites, burned to the ground or destroyed in the course of wars and battles. Consider the trail of destruction wrought by General Sherman in his march through Georgia. It would be an interesting challenge to trace the line of march by hunting for artifacts.

As land was exhausted by improper cultivation and dependence on a single crop, houses and supporting buildings deteriorated into disrepair. It was often easier to abandon the farm and move on to virgin land. Crop rotation, contour plowing, and soil conservation were then unheard of, and the practice of scientific farming lay many years in the future. The philosophy

Site of an old farmstead, marked by a chimney. *(Photo by Michael Hudoba)*

of colonial agriculture was expressed well in the words of an anonymous farmer who summed up his farming career with pride for his industrious work, bragging, "I have worn out three farms in my lifetime."

The abandoned houses crumbled in decay, and over a century or two left no trace except for the rubble of a chimney or the rough outline of a foundation. Grown over with weeds, vines, and briars—nature's process of healing the earth—such dwellings will only be discovered by chance or perceptive observation.

There are some clues which may facilitate the discovery of such a site. You may see the faint traces of a plowed furrow that has been eroded to barely perceptible humps of earth showing through the underbrush in a discernible pattern. The faint sign of long-past cultivation merits a careful exploration of the entire area. There may be remnants of split rails or logs marking the fence line of the abandoned field. Depending on how much time had passed since the land was allowed to return to nature, the

Mill Springs Hill, northeast of Monticello, Kentucky. This historic old mill is still operated in the colonial tradition.

vegetation is likely to exhibit differences in growth and age. The trees will show varying sizes and maturity between the formerly cleared land and the forest or woods' edge.

This type of observation could lead to discovery of a homesite. A patch of younger trees standing in the midst of more mature trees indicates a manmade clearing. It may have resulted from a timbering operation, but it is still worth examining for signs of a building foundation.

Another type of clue to look for is vegetation, shrubs, or trees that are inconsistent with the immediate environment. While the chance dropping of a seed from landscape plants by a bird or animal may account for isolated domestic plants in the wild, the presence of such domesticated planting almost certainly marks the immediate area of a long forgotten homesite.

Having found such a site, you should give the area a detailed search and proceed to study the site to plan your digging. A metal detector could lead you to the object of your exploration.

6

Hunting Settler Artifacts

DURING THE EARLY COLONIAL PERIOD, English colonists concentrated in the coastal areas and the estuaries of navigable rivers. They settled and farmed an area hemmed in by the Appalachian Mountain chain to the west. The French had established and reinforced their claims to the territory along the St. Lawrence River, the Great Lakes, and the Mississippi River—to the north and the west of the English colonies. The well-fortified northern and central French areas were known as New France, while the territory at the southern end of the Mississippi was named Louisiana. The French did not farm, depending instead on the fur trade and the fishing.

The barriers of mountains and the hostile French and Indians kept the colonists more or less confined, tied to their lines of communication and trade with England and the Old World. The fur trappers and intrepid frontiersmen who penetrated into territory beyond the Appalachians brought back reports of land rich in game, rivers teeming with fish, and virgin earth awaiting the plow.

Since the French used their territory as a resource for fur-bearing game, they established trading posts as their principal type of settlement. Detroit, New Orleans, and Mobile originally were French trading posts. The French voyageurs penetrated beyond the Great Lakes to Ontario, Wisconsin, and Minnesota and into and down the Mississippi River drainage in search of new areas for trapping. They used their scattered campsites only for short periods of time while in transit. The most likely spots to look for any possible evidence of such presence would be in the vicinity of the rapids of the voyageurs' water trails. Here they would pause to rest and plan for the inevitable portages around dangerous or impassable waters. Artifacts which might be found would include those items that were overlooked or lost in making or breaking camp or abandoned to lighten the load for portage. It is possible that a cache of trade goods, long forgotten or left behind by an exploring party that met disaster, may still await discovery.

The restless, the dissatisfied, and the adventurous among the English colonists pushed away from the established centers toward the backcountry and began to crowd the Indians, who retaliated by raiding and burning the backwoods homesteads. The Indians were encouraged by the French, who traded for furs with them and who had been waging a 150-year struggle against the British for control of the North American continent.

The conflict came to a head in the French and Indian War of 1754–1760, the resolution of three previous wars between England and France. The British won and gained control of all the French-held land east of the Mississippi. George Washington, who served with British troops along with other colonists, gained experience in wilderness warfare and a knowledge of British tactics which proved useful to him in the struggle to win the American Revolution.

When Napoleon, emperor of France, closed the port of New Orleans in 1802, President Thomas Jefferson became alarmed. He sent James Monroe to Paris to negotiate for the purchase of New Orleans; the adjacent Spanish lands to the east known as West Florida, which Napoleon had acquired from Spain in 1800;

and the territory France still held west of the Mississippi, reaching from the Gulf of Mexico to Canada and westward to the Rocky Mountains.

Napoleon was absorbed in war with England and his treasury was being depleted rapidly. He realized it would be difficult to hold the territory in the New World. Napoleon's offer to sell the area of one million square miles for $15,000,000 was readily accepted by President Jefferson. The Louisiana Purchase, as the transaction was called, ended French claims in 1803 on the North American continent and added a huge area of virgin land to the emerging United States of America.

As of 1776 there had been two and one-half million people in the colonies. They already had begun to reproduce some of the Old World social and economic patterns with their class distinctions. The restless spirit that had brought the colonists to the New World, along with a deep drive for self-assertion and the need to carve out a place for themselves and their families, made the frontier to the west an inviting challenge.

When the French domination of the western frontier was eliminated, the westward push gained strength. Settlers carried the frontier across the Alleghenies deep into the heartland of America. Kentucky and Tennessee had earlier become states, and Ohio followed in 1803.

The movement into the backwoods and wilderness was full of danger. It was not so much danger from wild animals, for the carnivorous species that might have been a threat to man were few in numbers, but the danger lay with unfriendly Indians.

While the colonists had been few in number and more or less localized in their settlements, the Indians had been helpful and taught them the old ways of survival in the new environment. But as the white man ventured into the backwoods and began to carve away at the wilderness to build log cabins and clear land for his crops, the Indians began to resent the encroachment of their traditional hunting and fishing territory. The settlers were competing with the Indians for the same game, and their habitations disrupted the ecological system that had supported the abundant wildlife.

The older half of Frankfort, Kentucky, hugs the northern bank of the Kentucky River. This river port was intended for exporting goods to Louisiana. (*Photo by Department of Public Information, Frankfort, Kentucky*)

The French also foresaw the potential threat of the backwoods settlers to their territorial aspirations and competition for the fur-bearing animals that was their principal resource. The French encouraged their fur trading partners to resist the intrusions of the English settlers. Indian raiding and marauding parties preyed on the isolated homesteads in the wilderness.

You can still find evidence of these backwoods tragedies scattered in the foothills of the Appalachians, a stone fireplace chimney standing as the only remains of the log cabin. Not all these remnants of backwoods homes were the result of Indian raiding parties. Whenever the pioneer settler felt that things were getting crowded, he was inclined to pack up and move on, abandoning his crude cabin to the ravages of time.

Chimney of a colonial backwoods cabin, not visible from any roadway.
(Photo by Michael Hudoba)

The backwoods settlers were self-sufficient and lived a frugal life with few luxury goods. They worked the land with their rifles by their sides. Tools were simple: an ax for clearing land and gathering firewood, a plow and cultivating hoe, basic items for rough carpentry, and special tools fashioned to accomplish individual needs. Furnishings were handmade and utilitarian, and kitchen utensils were basically simple: iron cookware, wooden kitchenware, and possibly a treasured set of pewter plates. A spinning wheel and loom were used to make clothing. Their total possessions were scanty and could be carried on their backs or with a horse and wagon. A move to a new location was uncomplicated.

The artifact hunter is not likely to find a large quantity of artifacts on the site around the stone chimneys, but it is still worth exploring. Here the metal detector is a most useful aid to reveal any iron or metal objects that may have been lost or overlooked. The tools of the backwoodsmen and wilderness settlers were treasured by their owners; only when they were totally worn out were they abandoned.

Fortunate is the artifact hunter who finds any tool of these early Americans. These basic tools, the ax and the plow, in the hands of determined, hard-working, and courageous men facing the hardships and perils of the frontier, laid the foundation for and helped to expand our nation. These relics of early America carry a very special meaning which serves to remind us that it was the hard work of individuals which combined to give strength and character to our United States.

7

Hunting Pioneer Artifacts

BY THE BEGINNING OF THE 1800s, many small farms were suffering from dwindling crop yields due to one-crop farming and overuse of the land. The resultant hard times, along with reports of the availability of rich land beyond the frontier, encouraged the farmers' desire to move westward beyond the Appalachians.

After the Louisiana Purchase, the migration developed into a great movement westward. The vast acreage of fertile land in the Mississippi River drainage from the Great Lakes to the Gulf of Mexico began attracting pioneers in large numbers.

Little was known of the lands to the west of the Mississippi River. Captain Robert Gray, an American navigator, had sailed up the Columbia River in the Pacific Northwest in 1792. The reports of trappers and fur traders indicated that the source of the Missouri River was in the mountains of the Far West, but an overland trail still had to be blazed.

President Thomas Jefferson, instrumental in the consummation of the Louisiana Purchase despite critical objections, wanted to know more about the lands west of the Mississippi River. He was successful in obtaining an appropriation from Congress to finance an expedition to explore the newly acquired territory. Jefferson chose his secretary, Captain Meriwether Lewis, and William Clark to lead an expedition which they assembled near St. Louis during the winter of 1803–1804.

The plan of exploration was to ascend the Missouri River to its source, cross the Continental Divide, and descend the Columbia River to its mouth. The expedition consisted of the two leaders, Lewis and Clark; fourteen soldiers; nine frontiersmen from Kentucky; two French boatmen; and Clark's black servant, York.

They started up the Missouri on May 14, 1804, poling a 55-foot covered keelboat along with two small craft. On July 30 they reached the site where they held their first powwow with the Indians, naming the place Council Bluffs (Iowa).

On October 26 the party reached the camps of the Mandan Indians, and on a site near what is now Stanton, North Dakota, they built Fort Mandan, where the expedition spent the winter.

During the winter stopover, a husband and wife team was added to the expedition: Charbonneau, a French interpreter, and his Indian wife, Sacagawea, the sister of a Shoshone chief. She was a fortuitous addition to the expedition, proving invaluable to the explorations. Sacagawea knew the countryside and the Indians, and served as an interpreter.

In the spring of 1805, the keelboat was sent back to St. Louis with natural history specimens and reports for President Jefferson. The expedition continued up the Missouri in the canoes they had built during the winter, passing the mouth of the Yellowstone River on to the Great Falls in Montana. Following a laborious sixteen-mile portage around the falls, the party reached Three Forks, where three rivers met the Missouri. These were named the Madison, the Jefferson, and the Gallatin after the great colonial patriots.

The leaders of the expedition decided to follow the largest of the three forks, the Jefferson River, and proceeded into the

Fort Clatsop National Memorial, Oregon. A close-up of the Lewis and Clark salt cairn at Seaside. The expedition produced sorely needed salt by boiling ocean water. *(Photo by Jack Boucher, National Park Service, U.S. Department of the Interior)*

country of the Shoshone, Sacagawea's people. Here they met the tribe whose chief was Sacagawea's brother. He supplied horses and guides to assist them in crossing the imposingly high Bitterroot Range of the Continental Divide. Reaching the Clearwater River, the party again built canoes, descended to the Lewis (now the Snake) River, and paddled down the Columbia, where they built a stockade, Fort Clatsop, now the site of a national memorial.

The following spring the exploration started to retrace its way eastward. In the Bitterroot Valley, Lewis and Clark separated to explore and learn more about the country.

Clark made his way to the Yellowstone River and followed it back to the Missouri River. Lewis, with nine men, headed toward the northeast to explore a branch of the Missouri which he named Marias. At Fort Mandan the parties were reunited and the expedition returned to St. Louis on September 23, 1806, after a journey that covered six thousand miles and lasted two years and four months.

Lewis and Clark brought back a great deal of new material for map makers. They also provided the basis for a United States claim to the Oregon territory. Their travel route was followed by American pioneers in covered wagons.

The Lewis and Clark expedition is considered the most important event in the development of the western United States. There is legislation pending in Congress to establish a Lewis and Clark Trail within a National Trails System. The proposed Lewis and Clark National Historic Trail would cover some thirty-seven hundred miles, following the complete route of the expedition. The trail begins near St. Louis and is primarily on water, along the Missouri, Snake, and Columbia rivers. It crosses portions of Missouri, Kansas, Nebraska, Iowa, South Dakota, North Dakota, Montana, Idaho, Oregon, and Washington, and terminates at the mouth of the Columbia River.

What a prize it would be for an enterprising artifact hunter exploring segments of the Lewis and Clark route to discover a campsite and artifact that could be authenticated as having belonged to the expedition!

The majority of pioneers were farmers whose desire for new land was insatiable. There was unrest and poverty in Europe, and the reports of opportunities to own land in the New World and to gain freedom from oppression began to attract waves of immigrants to America. The population of the interior expanded, and many new states joined the Union.

The pattern of selecting a home site was fairly standard and depended entirely on a favorable environment. The pioneer settler needed to find a fairly level spot that could be cleared for farming and that was near a dependable source of water, either a spring, stream, or river. Trees were needed to build a cabin and supply firewood. The great valleys to the west, with their fertile river bottomland and abundant game, offered the essentials needed for pioneers to establish new settlements.

The Indians, however, had long used the same locations on their annual migrations to their hunting grounds and so, almost inevitably, the Indians and pioneers found themselves in conflict over the possession of choice territory.

The Indians sought to maintain their traditional pattern of freedom of movement to obtain food by hunting and fishing; the pioneers sought to establish permanent communities. The same type of conflict developed in later years when the pioneer homesteaders began to stake out claims on the wide open cattle ranges and Indian lands further west.

There is no way to determine how many homesites were burned out or abandoned as a result of such confrontations. An artifact hunter, searching for the type of environment suitable for a home site and watching for the signs of habitation described in the previous chapter on settlers, may discover evidence of remains of a pioneer's presence, along with artifacts of that period of history.

The first trails from the settled colonies across the Appalachians toward the west generally followed Indian trails and waterways once used by trappers and traders that later were pounded into crude roads by pioneer settlers, who cleared brush and trees to make way for their wagons. Crude bridges were

Cumberland Gap, a former key gateway of westward movement. Pioneers once thrived here. *(Photo by Jack Boucher, National Park Service, U.S. Department of the Interior)*

built over unfordable streams, and logs were laid side by side to form a corduroy road over swampy places. These roads were miserable to travel; heavy use kept them in such bad shape that wet weather travel was hardly possible. About the only good time to negotiate the roads was during winter when they were frozen.

The pioneers who settled in Kentucky and Tennessee came largely from the old South and Pennsylvania, following one road that ran south and west from Richmond, Virginia, and another known as the Great Valley Road that joined it near Fort Chissel. From this junction the famed Wilderness Road cut by Daniel Boone and his men ran through the Cumberland Gap and across Kentucky to Louisville. This was the most important road serving as a gateway to the West. A branch road west of Fort Chissel led south and west to Knoxville and on to Nashville. It was joined east of Knoxville by the Jonesboro Road that stretched across North Carolina from New Bern on the coast.

The pioneer settlers from the middle states could follow the Great Valley Road or use one of the two military roads built during the French and Indian War—the Forbes Road, connecting Philadelphia with Pittsburgh, and Braddock's Road, running from Baltimore to Pittsburgh.

The New England settlers moving westward followed a single road running west from Boston. It divided into two branches at the Connecticut River, one going north to join the Mohawk Turnpike and the Great Genessee Road across northern New York toward Lake Erie, and the other branching southwest to connect with the Catskill Road leading to the headwaters of the Susquehanna River. The Genessee Road followed the south shore of Lake Erie across the Western Reserve on to the southern tip of Lake Michigan and continued southwestward to Vandalia, Illinois.

The Erie Canal, a pioneer engineering feat, was begun in 1817 and formally opened in the fall of 1825. It connected the Hudson River near Albany, New York, with Lake Erie at Buffalo. This was a major factor in the development of the region and movement westward.

Fort Pulaski National Monument at Savannah Beach, Georgia, an early nineteenth-century fort with a moat. *(Photo by Cecil W. Stoughton, National Park Service, U.S. Department of the Interior)*

The migrations into the rich lands of the lower south followed either the Upper Road along the Piedmont from Virginia to Columbus, Georgia, or the Fall Line Road from the Tidewater to Columbus, and then on from Columbus to Mobile, Alabama, and Natchez, Mississippi. The pioneers from Kentucky and Tennessee, moving on to new lands in the south, used roads that linked Lexington, Kentucky; Nashville; and Knoxville with Memphis; Natchez; Tuscaloosa and Florence, Alabama; and New Orleans.

These early trails leading into the backwoods and the frontier developed into a network of wagon roads, along which settlements sprang up and grew into villages and cities. Many of our modern highways and railroads follow the courses of these early roads, connecting the modern cities that emerged from the backwoods villages.

Today, although highway construction has routed roads

around metropolitan areas, segments of the old roads still remain, retaining many of their early physical characteristics. Exploring them is easy and fun; simply take an exit from the superhighway and drive into the countryside.

Valuable reference sources for planning such explorations are the files and back issues of local newspapers. Such early issues are certain to be filled with stories of local events of historical interest and descriptions of community people, all written in a quaint, old-fashioned style. Read the issues for clues to possible destinations for artifact hunting trips.

A brief newspaper item led me to one of the most informative and delightful interviews I've ever enjoyed. The story mentioned the celebration of a birthday party for a 94-year-old woman. I called her and arranged to talk with her. She was charming, alert, and possessed a superb memory. She recalled her childhood experiences during the Civil War battles at Bull Run, Virginia—how she'd listened to the guns and canons and watched the troops move as the battle progressed. Her description of the postfighting scene on her parents' farm is unforgettable, and her memories of the placement of the troops and details of the countryside were vivid. Part of our history became alive for me while talking with her.

You need only take time to do some research on the history of the area you plan to explore. You can find old newspapers, publications, and references to local history in the library and in the historical society.

Covered Wagons

As the eastern United States became densely populated and the central section of the country settled, the vast territory west of the Mississippi became the last frontier open to the restless, adventurous, and those who had not yet found their dreams. The Lewis and Clark expedition reported on wide-open spaces where land was plentiful and available.

Fur trappers and traders had penetrated into and beyond the Rocky Mountains, and colorful mountain men such as Jim

Bridger blazed trails through Indian country. The movement westward that began about 1840 surged with the news of the gold discovery in California in 1848 and grew into the greatest gold rush in history. The largest single migration westward was that of the Mormons in 1847, seeking to escape persecution for their religious beliefs. They made their way to the Salt Lake valley in Utah where they established a thriving colony and their own way of life.

The covered wagon era was thus born. Trains of the Conestoga wagons and prairie schooners began the arduous and dangerous journey to the promised land of California and the Pacific Northwest. The covered wagon trails, originating at Independence, Missouri, the major gathering point, led toward South Pass, Wyoming, and then along the Snake River route to Oregon, and the Humboldt River path to California. The best southern route made its way to Santa Fe, New Mexico, and then along the Gila River to California.

The Oregon Trail followed a two thousand-mile route from Independence along the valleys of the Kansas, Little Blue, and North Platte Rivers to Fort Laramie, then through the Black Hills into the Sweetwater River valley, through the Wind River Mountains across the Big Sandy, and then following the Bear River to Soda Springs where the California Trail branched south. The Oregon route continued along the Snake River to Fort Boise, north across the Blue Mountains to the headwaters of the Columbia River. It is the same route now followed by the Union Pacific Railroad from the Bear River.

The Conestoga wagon was a product of necessity and the times. Its sturdy construction could withstand the jostling of the rugged terrain; it was capable of being floated across unfordable rivers; and its cover provided shelter for the women and children. It was large enough to carry the belongings of the seekers of a new home, as well as tools to build and seed to plant.

The covered wagon days took a heavy toll of the pioneer settlers. The journey was hazardous, the weather often inclement, and the climate dry and hostile. The Indians watched with apprehension as the pioneers began to invade their traditional hunting grounds and territory. At first they had been helpful to the intruders, but as the numbers increased and the buffalo and game herds were dispersed or wantonly slaughtered, the resentment of intrusion turned into open hostility. Wagon trains were raided and burned and the pioneers killed. There were not enough federal troops manning the scattered forts to protect the travelers.

The remnants of an ill-fated wagon train may still be hidden from view, awaiting discovery after these many years. What happened to the treasured belongings which were not burned? Did the members of the raiding party carry them off and, with their curiosity satiated, discard them in some out of the way place where an artifact hunter may find a link to these brave Americans of the past?

Homesteads

By 1850, California had achieved statehood, and the last of the frontier was settled. A vast area of the West became the domain of huge ranches that required open range to graze cattle. The arid climate produced only sparse vegetation, and it took as many as a hundred acres to sustain one cow. Water was scarce and vital to the ranches, which were built around waterholes, streams, rivers, and mountain sources of water. Water rights were a primary asset of the range, and the struggle to hold

Fort Union, New Mexico. Reenactment of western frontier Indian wars. *(Photo by Fred E. Mang, Jr., National Park Service, U.S. Department of the Interior)*

possession of the rights developed into a militant battle by the cattlemen.

Meanwhile, there were disputes over land possession in the Louisiana territory by pioneer settlers who claimed "squatter sovereignty" on the basis of occupation, regardless of the Homestead Act of 1862. The law provided that the head of a family could become the owner of 160 acres of land by residing on it and cultivating or improving it for three years. This opened the vast territory of public land west of the Mississippi River to homesteading.

The prospect of free land brought a migration of homesteaders to the open ranges in the west. The homesteaders needed water for their home sites and crop land. They staked out claims on land with water, built their homes, and fenced the land. The Indians, already hostile, felt that the homesteaders were the final irritant; the Indians retaliated by raiding, burning homes and crops, and killing the intruders. The cattlemen, finding their water holes fenced off, the open range becoming settled, and their way of life threatened, began to harass the homesteaders too, seeking to drive them from the land.

It was a trying period in the history of the settlement of this country. As in the backwoods of the East, where cabins were burned by warring Indians, so also in the West you may find evidence of burned-out and abandoned home sites marking the end of a dream for pioneer families, whose difficult journey was destined to end in tragedy.

Pioneer cabin remains. *(Photos by Michael Hudoba)*

8

Battlefields and Campaign Trails

SPORADIC WARS were fought on the new nation's soil, beginning with the French and Indian War in the late 1700s and culminating with the Civil War some hundred years later. The artifact hunter will find rich hunting on Civil War battlegrounds, but the more intrepid may wish to search for older and more difficult-to-find relics of earlier wars.

The most decisive conflict in the 150-year struggle between France and England broke out in 1754, when British troops under the leadership of George Washington sought to build a fort at the confluence of the Allegheny and Monongahela Rivers and were fired on by the French. Most of the fighting in the first three wars between France and England took place in the New England and New York areas, but the final war, known as the French and Indian War, broke out in the upper Ohio Valley and ranged from Pennsylvania through New York and into Quebec, where in 1760 the French capitulated with the surrender of Montreal.

The first battle of the American Revolution broke out fifteen years later in Massachusetts at Lexington and Concord, and another soon followed at Bunker Hill. Fierce fighting ranged across Pennsylvania during the winter of 1777–1778, with British victories along Brandywine Creek near Chadds Ford and Paoli, and the capture of Philadelphia. The Continental army suffered a winter of hardship and bitter cold at Valley Forge.

The turning point came when the Americans, during the course of three battles, turned back the attack of seven thousand British troops in upstate New York and forced British General John Burgoyne to surrender at Saratoga. The war seesawed back and forth during the next three years—1778 to 1781—with

Valley Forge, Pennsylvania, where George Washington and his army spent a severe winter during the American Revolution. *(Photo by Richard Frear, National Park Service, U.S. Department of the Interior)*

no clear advantages for either side. The Americans won a battle at Cowpens, South Carolina, inflicting heavy casualties on the British, forcing them to withdraw in early 1781 despite a victory at Guilford Courthouse at Greensboro, North Carolina. The fighting moved to Yorktown, Virginia, where in 1781 the British surrendered.

Another conflict with Great Britain, the War of 1812, produced more battlefields for the artifact hunter to explore, beginning with the British victory at Bladensburg, Maryland, and the brief occupation of the White House and U.S. Capitol. Land battles were fought at Fort Dearborn (now Chicago) and Detroit, and naval battles occurred on Lake Erie and Lake Champlain. At the war's end, Andrew Jackson defeated the British at New Orleans.

Bloodshed moved to the southwest in 1848, with the outbreak of a dispute with Mexico over the U.S. annexation of Texas. The Americans conquered California, New Mexico, and northern Mexico in this short-lived conflict.

But the bloodiest war yet to be fought began in 1861—the Civil War—when Confederate batteries at Charleston, South Carolina, fired on the Union-held Fort Sumter in the city harbor. Three months later, Confederate troops routed the Union army at Bull Run (Manassas), Virginia, in the first major battle of the war. The North and South then fought a series of indecisive engagements in Virginia and Maryland during the remainder of 1861.

The tide began to turn, however, when Northern forces tightened the blockade of the Confederacy and launched a successful drive to control the Mississippi River to New Orleans. The Confederacy was split and its armies forced out of Kentucky, western Tennessee, northern Mississippi, Missouri, and parts of Arkansas and Louisiana. The Union forces occupied the coast of Virginia, half of North Carolina, and parts of the Florida and Georgia coasts.

The main theater of war was Virginia, whose northern boundary faced the national capital across the Potomac and whose capital, Richmond, was barely a hundred miles to the south. The

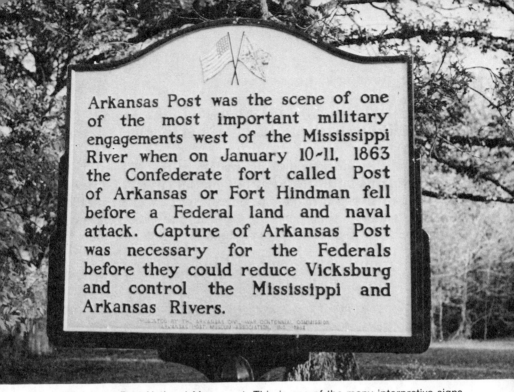

Arkansas Post was the scene of one of the most important military engagements west of the Mississippi River when on January 10-11, 1863 the Confederate fort called Post of Arkansas or Fort Hindman fell before a Federal land and naval attack. Capture of Arkansas Post was necessary for the Federals before they could reduce Vicksburg and control the Mississippi and Arkansas Rivers.

(Above) Arkansas Post National Monument. This is one of the many interpretive signs you will find along the nation's highways. *(Photo by Cecil W. Stoughton, National Park Service, U.S. Department of the Interior)*

(Below) Arkansas Post, Arkansas. Mule shoe, key with metal tag attached marked "27," and counterweight. *(Photo by M. Woodbridge Williams, National Park Service, U.S. Department of the Interior)*

Confederacy turned back a Union offensive against Richmond and advanced into the North, only to be stopped at Antietem, Maryland.

The Union expanded its wedge in the Mississippi Valley, driving its forces further south, but in Virginia General Robert E. Lee scored a major Confederate victory at Chancellorsville, frustrating a Union drive to flank him at Fredericksburg in an effort to cut him off from Richmond. The South then took the

Fredericksburg and Spotsylvania National Military Park. Cannon and battle map at Fairview, Chancellorsville battlefield. *(Photo by R. Happel, National Park Service, U.S. Department of the Interior)*

initiative, as Lee advanced northward to the Potomac where he penetrated the Union to Gettysburg, Pennsylvania. The battle of Gettysburg, fought from July 1 through July 3, 1863, was the most fiercely contested and decisive battle of the entire war. Lee lost, and the tide turned against the Confederacy.

General Sherman marched from Tennessee through Georgia to the Atlantic in 1864, splitting the eastern half of the Confederacy. Then, in 1865, as Sherman closed in on the Confederate rear, the Army of the Potomac advanced against Lee and forced him to abandon Richmond. Lee surrendered at Appomattox Court House, Virginia, on April 9, 1865.

The four-year war recorded some 2,200 battles and more than 6,800 engagements of all kinds within a fairly limited area of the nation. The war was thoroughly documented. By an act of Congress, official records of the Union and Confederate armies

Foundation remains of a Civil War period homestead. *(Photo by Michael Hudoba)*

and navies were compiled and printed by the U.S. Government Printing Office in Washington, D.C. The documents include every official dispatch and communication on a day-to-day basis and provide detail of every event and movement, including skirmishes and battles on both land and sea as reported by the participating officers.

The volumes are published in two sets, *Official Records of the Union and Confederate Navies in the War of the Rebellion* and *War of the Rebellion Official Records of the Union and Confeder-*

ate Armies. They are invaluable references for artifact hunters who wish to locate precisely the area of troop movements and naval operations. While these volumes are comparatively rare, they can be found in libraries with large reference collections.

To pinpoint more closely the exact locations of war events in your part of the country, you can use maps and sketches of battle positions and detailed notes logged by participants and observers. For copies, write the National Archives in Washington. In order to determine which maps to order, you need a key publication, "Civil War Maps in the National Archives," which describes the maps, locations, and ordering code reference numbers. You can order the publication (National Archives No. 64-12 or Library of Congress No. A64-7308) from the Superintendent of Documents, U.S. Government Printing Office, Washington, D.C. 20402.

These sources will probably provide you with more reference material on the Civil War than you will be able to use. Your local library will be able to supply even more. The Library of Congress is the ultimate source for all published reference material. Most people aren't aware that their senator or congressman can provide them with a Library of Congress bibliography on a particular subject. Historical societies also are likely to be quite helpful in providing information on Civil War battle sites.

Almost three and one-half million troops were involved in the Civil War fighting, and you can imagine the tremendous numbers of rounds of ammunition fired. That means that "mini balls" are likely to be found in the vicinity of any Civil War action. Every Civil War buff and artifact hunter has seen and collected these familiar lead bullets which over time have oxidized to grayness. Union bullets are rifled with three rings and Confederate with two rings. A specialized collection of mini balls would contain a variety of the calibers used by both sides

(Opposite page) A typical map available from the National Archives. Lines indicate Union and Confederate troop lines; Union artillery position is to the right of the village and Confederate troop lines are positioned on the prominent hill overlooking the village.

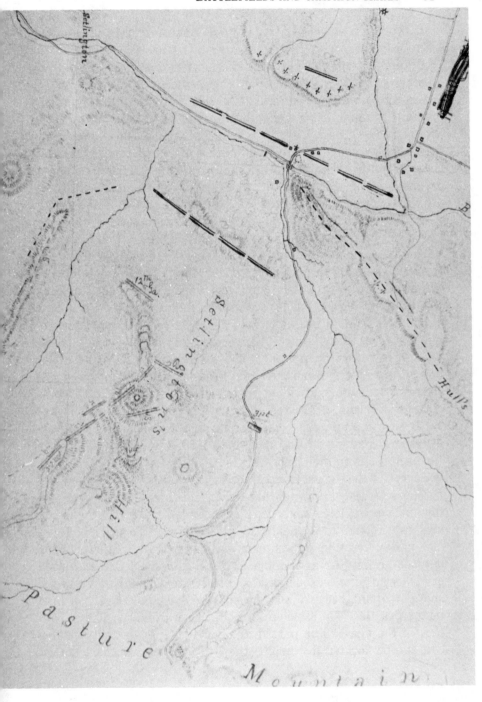

and would represent a variety of manufacturers, including European ones.

Equipment carried by the soldiers often was lost or discarded during a hectic movement or engagement, while making or breaking camp, or on a difficult march. You might look for such items if you plan to go artifact hunting on Civil War battlefields. They range from rifles to personal possessions, including bayonets, uniform buttons, canteens, belt and harness buckles, spurs, swords, coins, and other metal objects which were able to withstand the corrosion of time and the elements. Stanley Phillips' *Excavated Artifacts From Battle and Campsites of the Civil War* describes and illustrates individual objects.

If you plan to hunt for war relics, a metal detector is indispensable. There are a number of good ones on the market. Look for a model that can discriminate and eliminate trash items such as aluminum pulltabs, bottle caps, and candy foil. A good quality detector can signal the presence of a metal object deep in the ground. In some areas, however, metal detectors are not practical. For example, highly mineralized soil gives a signal strong enough to mask the presence of a metal object. With practice, you will be able to learn the capabilities of your own machine.

For more information on metal detectors, you might write Charles Garrett of Garrett Electronics, Garland, Texas. Garrett's firm manufactures metal detectors and has published an operating manual for the machines, and the firm is willing to field questions on their use.

Garrett strongly urges users of metal detectors to respect the outdoors. "Trespassing, tearing down fences and buildings, leaving uncovered holes, and other such offenses are causing landowners' protests to be heard by elected officials," Garrett says. He warns that the government will step in to regulate such outdoor activity unless hobbyists begin to respect private property. As an example, he says a coin hunter should never use a shovel to hunt because shovels cut the sod and leave holes. A better practice is to use a small knife or screwdriver. These tools permit the grass to be parted, the soil to be penetrated, and the coin to be located by touch, then flipped out of the ground.

Artifact hunters can apply similar techniques. If you must dig a hole, be sure to cover it up after removing the object of your search. This is no different than the requirement to replace a divot on the golf course. The thoughtless digger wears out his welcome in very short order.

While a haphazard search with a metal detector may yield the discovery of a Civil War artifact, a carefully planned search will be successful more often. One of the best Civil War artifact hunters I know is Kenneth Trobaugh. He not only gathered his own impressive collection of Civil War items, but also supplied the Confederate Museum in Front Royal with representative items for its collection.

Like other serious Civil War buffs, he carefully prepares for an exploratory search by studying references to troop activity that may have taken place in the vicinity of his artifact hunting locale. He has compiled his own reference library on the subject and has become an authority on troop movements, campaigns, and engagements in an area that he can drive to for weekend collecting. Through his study of Civil War records and dispatches, he has been able to locate campsites that had been long overlooked by casual searches.

An exploded Civil War shell. With patience and the sophisticated use of a metal detector, Kenneth Trobaugh was able to locate various parts and reconstruct the exploded shell. *(Photo by Kenneth Trobaugh)*

Trobaugh's artifacts are carefully and attractively mounted in frames which identify the location of the campsite where they were found. They include uniform buttons, spurs, bayonets, miniballs, buckles, and a variety of other items associated with soldiers and camps.

When Trobaugh finds and digs a Civil War artifact, he uses a stiff-bristled toothbrush to remove soil and material clinging to the surface. The objects are covered with rust, which he prefers not to remove, since it serves as a protective covering.

Trobaugh makes extensive use of a metal detector and he has become an expert in the use of this instrument. He upgrades his

Civil War artifacts from the Trobaugh collection. *(Photos by Kenneth Trobaugh)*

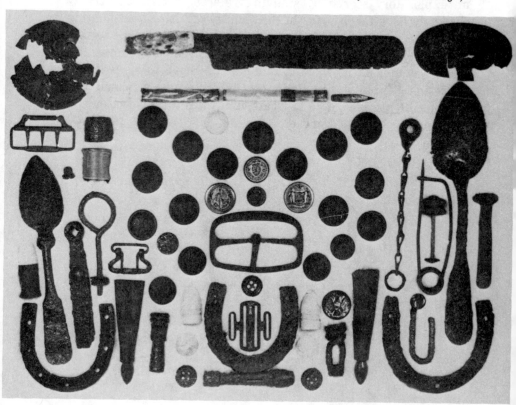

instruments as the manufacturer improves the models of his preference. As an illustration of his refined technique in the use of the machine, his collection includes an exploded Civil War shell that he reconstructed from its scattered fragments.

Trobaugh's technique in searching an area he believes to have been a campsite is to use a zigzag pattern with the detector

Civil War bullets from the Kenneth Trobaugh collection. *(Photos by Kenneth Trobaugh)*

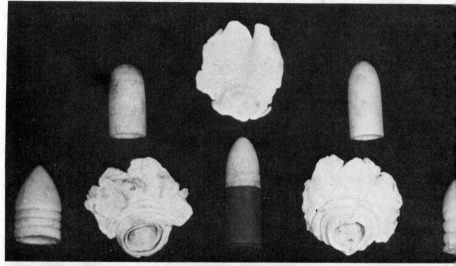

inches above the ground and with the discriminator finely tuned to reject signals of modern-day debris. Whenever he finds an artifact, he makes a thorough sweep of the area with the detector. A light sprinkle of white detergent powder at the point of each find marks the perimeters of the campsite. The next rain dissolves the powder, leaving the area in its original state.

Note the firing pin on the bottom right. This fit into the top of the shell. At bottom left is the lead casing for the base of the shell. Note the barrel rifling marks. *(Photo by Kenneth Trobaugh)*

Although he has conducted many fruitless explorations, his ratio of success because of careful preparation is high. He stresses the need to obtain the landowner's permission prior to exploring on private property and to cover up every hole that is dug.

Although an area may have been changed by human activity in the 114 years since the war, major features of the terrain will be the same and can serve as guideposts for blocking out your search. The curves and bends of a river, the joining of two rivers or streams, the configurations of the hills or shape of an individual hill, the valley or valleys between—all are landmarks that can help an observant eye locate the reference points described in a narrative or log of the scene of an engagement.

The battle position and troop movement maps available from the National Archives identify significant physical features of the terrain in relation to the position lines of the opposing troops. The map will approximate a closeup aerial view of the scene; it is often difficult to isolate a precise location from a ground-level scan of the terrain.

An important aid to use in conjunction with the Civil War map is a topographic map of the same area. These are prepared by the U.S. Geological Survey, Department of the Interior, Washington, D.C. The topographic map delineates the physical features of the terrain, progressive elevations of the land, roads, water courses, buildings, and details not shown on standard road maps. The Geological Survey publishes a state-by-state index from which you may obtain the code number for ordering the detailed quadrant maps of the areas you wish to explore.

You also should look for the familiar highway marker which identifies the general route of march of troops toward the site of a Civil War battlefield. Museums associated with national and historical sites also are excellent sources of data relating to events that took place nearby.

To chart the course of a line of movement, you need to determine what might have been the most expeditious route between two known reference points. Troops in full movement with cannon and supply wagons needed terrain favorable to transporting heavy equipment; cavalry was limited only by the capability of the horse; and movement of the foot soldier was adaptable to most any terrain.

With certain notable exceptions, there were comparatively few extended sieges. The Civil War was one of movement and maneuvering for position. These tactics called for the extensive use of hastily set-up campsites and bivouacs. The need to change position invariably meant haste in gathering equipment; in confusion many items were lost or overlooked. Such campsites with their hidden artifacts await discovery.

There are many collectors of Civil War relics and memorabilia. A recent Civil War show in Fairfax, Virginia, attracted enough buffs and collectors to rent 125 tables to display their collections for trading and selling. Such shows also are held in Fredericksburg and Winchester, Virginia; Harpers Ferry, West Virginia; and Gettysburg, Pennsylvania.

9

Treasures in Old Privies

INDOOR PLUMBING is a comparatively new luxury, and many of us remember cold walks down the path to the outhouse, part of a way of life that has virtually disappeared in this country. Privies and wells were essential parts of colonial households and early American homes. Privies were also used as convenient garbage dumps, since no communities had municipal garbage or waste-gathering programs. Along with kitchen wastes, anything that was broken or had outlived its usefulness was dumped into the privy. Similarly, whenever a water well ran dry or turned bad, the shaft of the well was used as a catchall for rubbish.

You might turn up your nose at the thought of searching for artifacts in old privies, but think again. Organic matter is rapidly recycled by bacteria, earthworms, and other minute forms of life into nutrients that revitalize the soil.

Take, for example, this story about Alexandria, one of Virginia's oldest cities and George Washington's home town. Before construction began on a new courthouse on a deteriorated city block, the archaeological commission sought permission and an appropriation from the city and the National Park Service to explore the area. Some two hundred years before, the block had been a thriving commercial center with a smokehouse, silversmith shop, bakery, several taverns, and an opera house.

Plans for exploring the area were developed after researching historical documents, property surveys, wills, and other records that provided clues to the placement of buildings on the site.

The most productive sources of artifacts, once the excavation began, were old privies and wells which had served the homes and shops. As the excavation went deeper, each succeeding level produced artifacts of different historical periods, not unlike excavations of ancient civilizations whose cities were built one on top of the other over the centuries. The digging in Alexandria has attracted volunteer archaeology and history buffs who supply the labor for the project.

Loose material is dug and hauled out of excavated pits— formerly wells and privies—in buckets. The contents are spread on a screen suspended over a dumpster and washed down with a hose to clear off the soil. The contents remaining on the screen are sorted into categories—glass and metal objects, leather and textile remnants. They are placed in plastic bags, labeled by feature and the depth level where found. Analysis of these materials will unfold a great deal of information about the lives of the early residents of that city block. When the digging is completed and the information is analyzed, the most valuable objects will be collected for exhibits.

It is possible that the Alexandria archaeological project may someday serve as a pilot for other cities of great historic background. Urban renewal projects designed to restore deteriorated sections of our old cities should be preceded by an examination of possible archaeological interest in the project site.

Artifact hunters in the future will no doubt have a field day sifting through the trash of our twentieth century throwaway culture. We accumulate, consume, and discard huge volumes of goods. Mass production has created the ultimate in disposable consumer goods. You can imagine how appalled the early Americans, who lived frugally and used everything thoroughly, would be to see the useful objects that we so casually toss into the waste can. Countless truckloads are hauled to central disposal sites daily, and these eventually are covered over with earth to create manmade hills. The modern-day earthen mounds are reminiscent of the work of the Indian mound builders whose burial sites contained the earthly goods and treasures of their time.

During the eighteenth and nineteenth centuries, before the development of central community waste disposal services, villages and communities used common dumping sites, usually located in eroded gullies or over the side of an embankment. A resident whose home was surrounded by a plot of land might bury his waste in a series of pits. If you learn to spot such pits, you can find clues to early habitation. Watch the color of the soil. Topsoil is finely textured and dark; beneath it is a layer of thicker, less friable subsoil, usually of a different color. This contrasting subsoil finds its way to the surface of refilled holes or is found scattered around the excavation site.

Farm families disposed of their rubbish in gullies or behind out of the way embankments and usually did not bother to cover it up with soil. Eventually the rubbish piles became overgrown with briars and trees. Organic matter disappeared, and tin cans and light metal objects deteriorated by rust, leaving only minute traces. More substantial metal objects, however, accumulated a protective coating of rust and retained their original forms. These objects are targets for artifact hunters. The most indestructible materials found in such dumping grounds are objects made of glass, pottery, and china. Glass bottles and containers of every description were used extensively in the course of everyday life. When the contents were emptied, the bottle was discarded. With the exception of slight changes in tone of color, these bottles remain unchanged over the years.

Glassmaking was one of the earliest crafts introduced to colonial America. The first colony in Jamestown in 1607 produced glass, although no known examples have been identified positively as having originated there. Most of what we know as early American glass was made after 1800, and much of it was produced after 1850.

If you are fortunate enough to discover an undisturbed old dumping site, you will likely find a mother lode of collectible glass bottles, with the possibility that among them will be a valuable and highly prized specimen. It is exhilarating to search an old dumping site, for you may anticipate unearthing various collectible items that will reveal clues to the life-style of the household and era in which they were used.

You may discover the remains of a habitation site, such as the outline of a foundation or the crumbling ruins of a house, while on an exploration trip. Carefully appraise the immediate vicinity for the logical location of other buildings associated with home sites. Look at the surface of the earth. A different type of vegetation will be found on earth packed down by years of footsteps or on an area once covered by a structure. An area with deep gullies or land too rocky or steep for cultivation may once have been a dump site.

Pick up an old tin can. Does it have telltale rust spots? What about that old bottle? Has it been exposed to the weather? Use your metal detector to reveal buried objects. Clear a path into the bramble patch with a machete. Unless you are a specialist, be alert on any exploration trip to a variety of clues that suggest the earlier presence of man.

In my boyhood, I made a discovery in an out of the way

An old iron furnace, east of Cumberland Gap. *(Photo by Ralph H. Anderson, National Park Service, U.S. Department of the Interior)*

woodland in Ohio. Hidden under a dense growth of vines built into a hillside was a stone arch with a cave-like opening. Scattered around the base, hidden under a thick accumulation of leaves, were lumps of rainbow-colored, glass-like stones, which turned out to be slag. I had found the location of an iron furnace that dated to 1803 and had been abandoned and forgotten long before. The discovery was a thrill I will never forget, though I have no way of knowing how many others may have been there before me. The site is now commemorated by a historical marker and I take personal pleasure in reading its legend.

Oddly enough, I made a similar discovery years later on a float fishing trip through the pine woods wilderness in New Jersey. On an exploratory walk into the woods I found a brilliantly colored, glass-like lump of slag. It reminded me of my boyhood find, and I learned later that there had been an iron furnace in the vicinity which dated back to the Revolution.

A number of iron making sites supplied the forges of colonial America. Most of them have been located and marked for their historical significance, but there could be undiscovered ones awaiting you. Iron ore is common and the construction of a primitive furnace—not much more than an extra large fireplace built to ensure maximum airflow through the flue—was simple.

Iron was a key material in colonial and pioneer America. Ironworkers and blacksmiths made heavy and durable tools, such as axes, plows, nails, wagon parts, and forms for other essentials. A simple forge, anvil, and hammer were essential equipment for any farm, until modern production methods began to provide an array of finished products. The pioneers and later farmers were adept at repairing and maintaining their equipment with a basic ability at the forge.

A visit to an old farmstead likely will turn up the rusted hulks of horse-drawn farm machinery, retired in favor of tractor-powered equipment. Old wagon wheels and iron wheels from such machinery have been salvaged by artifact hunters and often are used as decorative items. Iron seats from horse-drawn machinery also are much sought-after items. Though the drive to salvage all kinds of metal during World War II sent some of

Remains of an old wagon. *(Photo by Michael Hudoba)*

the retired farm equipment to the melting furnaces, there is still worn-out and obsolete farm machinery rusting away in the back corners of every older farm.

If you plan to look in such areas, be sure to ask permission first and be prepared to negotiate to salvage parts from such equipment. Older farm owners, having experienced the transition from horse-drawn to tractor-powered machinery, may retain a sentimental attachment to those worn-out pieces of equipment. They remember the long hours in the hot sun using them, or the times they repaired and nursed it in order to finish urgent farm chores.

10

The Recent Past

DURING THE LATE 1800s and early 1900s, the Great Lakes states went through a massive exploitation of their abundant woodland resources. Hundreds of thousands of acres were cleared of trees, leaving a barren landscape of tree stumps as far as the eye could see. Some of this land was cleared for farming, and some was replanted with trees and turned into national forests. Timber companies moved on to the Pacific Northwest. Campsites where lumberjacks lived during the timber-cutting operations may still be found in Maine and New England, the Great Lakes states, and the Pacific Northwest. A town which depended totally on lumbering was destined to become a ghost town when the supply of trees was exhausted.

The timber was moved to the lumber mills by floating great rafts of logs down rivers during spring high water. Horses dragged logs into staging areas to await the floodwaters of spring thaw. You may search such locations for relics of former lumbering days. Many of these rivers now are prized trout

Indian artifacts found by Michael Hudoba on fishing trips. All these artifacts were exposed to the open; no digging took place. *(Photo by Michael Hudoba)*

fishing waters, and you might combine an artifact hunting excursion with a fishing trip.

Other fascinating eras from our recent history provide rich hunting grounds for artifacts. The first transcontinental railroad linking the east and west coasts was completed in 1869, with the ceremonial last spike driven into the last tie at Promontory Point, Utah. Campsites of the workers who built the railroad followed the line of tracks in leapfrog fashion as it advanced. Tracing the construction of the railroads through artifacts found in such camps is an interesting challenge for both railroad buffs and artifact hunters.

The cattle drives from Texas to the railheads at Abilene, Kansas, are unique events in American history and could provide hours of enjoyable hunting for the artifact hound. The Chisholm Trail, made famous in story, is the best known of the old cattle drive trails. If the subject interests you, the library can provide information on more obscure routes.

During my wanderings in the Rocky Mountains and in California, I was fascinated by the ghost towns left behind when the veins of gold and silver ore were exhausted or lost to faults in the earth. Exploring ghost towns has a large following among artifact hunters, who have swept through ghost-town areas with armies of metal detectors. Sites of old mines are readily apparent if you look for tailings that stream down the hillsides from the old mine entrances. A placer mining operation will have left behind great mounds of tailings. Campsites are almost sure to have accompanied most mining sites, and these offer exploration opportunities.

Many relics were abandoned along the torturous trail into the Klondike during the Alaska gold rush of 1897.

I once had an unforgettable interview with a character I encountered in my role as an artifact hunter. A stranger who said he had read something I had written called and insisted upon coming to talk with me. He aroused my curiosity by mentioning the frontier cattle town, Abilene. I agreed to see him.

He arrived—a slight and aged man with penetrating blue eyes sunk deep in a wrinkled face, which was partially hidden by a drooping white mustache. The man laid a matched pair of .44 Colt Frontier Pistols side by side on the table.

"These are for sale," he said. "I want you to have them."

With that, he began to tell the story of his life on the frontier, how he had carried the pistols, and of the gun fights he had survived.

"You know," he mused, "the old-time gun fighters could draw fast enough, but they were lousy shots. They couldn't hit a washtub at 40 feet."

He chuckled. "All you had to do was to take the time to aim."

The Colt .44s were authentic. And my visitor looked the part that his narrative portrayed.

Artifact hunting can be more, you see, than a simple search for relics, mementos, and objects from the past. It also can become an adventure in tracing and savoring some of the experiences of people who helped to settle and build our nation.

11

Nostalgia Artifacts

AN ARTIFACT HUNTER, equipped with a metal detector and armed with informational clues, is likely to be tempted by visions of hidden treasure troves. It is estimated that half of the refined gold in the world still lies at the bottom of the sea, much of it lost by Spanish treasure ships loaded with loot gathered in the New World sunk by Caribbean hurricanes off the coast of Florida.

Stories of pirates' treasure chests buried on the Atlantic and Pacific coastal shores are intriguing and have basis in fact. There are beaches on both coasts that yield coins and artifacts washed up by waves after heavy storms.

Buried treasure also is associated with wars. News of an impending raid or invasion by enemy troops sent people scurrying to bury their family silverware and coins for safekeeping. Looting often took place after raids or battles and the looters sometimes hid or buried what they took in order not to hamper their escape. Many never returned to the site, and the treasure remains hidden.

People who lived in remote areas—farmers, for example—didn't trust banks in the past and sometimes buried their coins and money or hid them in postholes. You may be fortunate enough to locate coins with your metal detector while you are searching an area. Among them are likely a few whose numismatic worth exceeds face value.

The possibility of finding hidden treasure is especially tantalizing to adventurous artifact hunters. Several books describe treasure hunting as a specialty, and you can get maps that purport to lead to such hidden caches. For 30¢ you can obtain a publication called "A Descriptive List of Treasure Maps and Charts in the Library of Congress" (Catalog No. 64-60033) from the Superintendent of Documents, U.S. Government Printing Office, Washington, D.C. Another publication available from the same source for $1.25, lists maps showing explorers' routes, trails, and early roads in the United States (Catalog No. 62-60066).

Whether you search for Indian relics or artifacts from the Civil War, the frontier, or some other period, is probably dependent upon the part of the country in which you live and its archaeology and history. The first artifacts you discover may lead you to a specialized collection of objects related to those initial finds. The first find is a tipoff that other artifacts from the same period are likely to be found nearby.

Today there's a great fascination with nostalgia, the artifacts of the recent past. Americana has attracted large numbers of new hobbyists and collectors who own collections of every conceivable object made and used in everyday life in the recent past.

You can find antique shops in every city. Larger metropolitan areas usually have sections of the city devoted almost exclusively to antiques. It would take a week, for example, to visit every antique shop in New Orleans, New York, or Chicago. The result would be a liberal education in the types of artifacts that are prized enough to occupy selling space in commercial establishments.

Don't overlook flea markets as sources of artifacts. Many of the entrepreneurs who exhibit are artifact hunters who devote part of their time to exploring for items of their specialized interest. A visit to a thriving flea market will provide you with considerable information about the types of artifacts to be found in your location and will reveal the extensive variety of artifacts currently being collected.

Talk with the owners of various displays. It is likely that they started out as artifact hunters and that the hobby turned their interest to the specialities which they have collected in sufficient numbers to make available for sale.

Glass has been produced from colonial times, and its current use has expanded. Bottles are among the most common artifacts to be found. They span the historical periods of our country— they can be found in Civil War campsites, old lumber and mining camp locations, everywhere that man has worked and lived. The variety of shapes, styles, and uses of bottles makes them highly collectible. There are many bottle collectors' clubs. A good introductory publication on the subject is *The Award Guide to Collecting Bottles*, by Nancy Pratt Berkow.

As mentioned earlier, a turn-of-the-century dumping site will yield what could amount to the beginning of a collection of bottles. Digging at such a site requires caution: there will be broken glass and sharp metal edges. Care in sifting through the earth must be exercised and protective gloves should be worn.

Fences played a key role in the settlement of our country and the invention of barbed wire led to some historic confrontations between homesteaders and cattlemen. Collecting the various types of barbed wire manufactured over the years may interest you. You can find remnants of barbed wire by wandering through backwoods areas. Sections up to a foot and a half long will be just fine.

Children's toys also are prized by collectors. Those made of metal may be found among discarded items in old dumps.

In reality, everything that humans have used in years gone by is part of the vast array of artifacts that are collectible.

Various types of bottles excavated at Fort Union, New Mexico.
(Photo by Fred E. Mang, Jr., National Park Service, Regional Archeologist's Office.)

Appendix A

Historical and Archaeological Resources

THE BUILDING AND CONSTRUCTION of roads, dams, airports, shopping centers, and residential communities has inadvertently flooded, buried, or destroyed irreplaceable archaeological resources. When these links and clues to our past are lost, pages of potential information are left forever blank.

It is only comparatively recently that any definitive recognition of the value of our historic and archaeological resources has been acknowledged in programs established by federal and state laws. There is a long way to go before such recognition will be implemented effectively.

The Society for American Archaeology, 1703 New Hampshire Avenue, N.W., Washington, D.C. 20009 has a booklet available for 40¢, titled "Archaeology and Archaeological Resources."

The Committee on the Public Understanding of Archaeology of the Society of American Archaeology has a representative in each state who can answer questions about archaeology and provide information about meetings, museums, activities, and programs in the state. For information and to be put on their mailing list write the Committee on the Public Understanding of Archaeology, University of Arkansas Museum, Fayetteville, AK 72701.

"Locating archaeological resources and recording them in such a way that they can be evaluated requires systematic reconnaissance of an area," a Committee publication advises. "Unlike many of our historic buildings, most prehistoric and many historic sites have been literally lost to human knowledge and must be rediscovered. In only a few small regions of the country have there been adequate surveys by archaeologists. Sites recorded by this survey work are on file with state agencies and, in some instances, are on the National Register. However, most of the United States has not been thoroughly or professionally surveyed for archaeological resources, and in most areas sites on record are only those that have been discovered during cursory studies, by accident, or that have been reported to responsible agencies by the public."

As an artifact hunter in the pursuit of your hobby, you may hope to discover clues that will reveal the location of a significant site worthy of listing as part of our national heritage. Such a possibility adds zest to the adventures of exploration.

The National Register is a listing maintained by the National Park Service of architectural, historical, archaeological, and cultural sites of local, state, or national significance. Copies of the National Register may be obtained from the Superintendent of Documents, U.S. Government Printing Office, Washington, D.C. 20402.

A federal law, The Historic Preservation Act of 1966, affects archaeological sites. The preamble to this law deserves quotation: "That the spirit and direction of the Nation are founded upon and reflected in its historic past:

"That the historical and cultural foundations of the nation should be preserved as a living part of our community life and development in order to give a sense of orientation to the American people:

"That, in face of ever-increasing extensions of urban center, highways, and residential, commercial, and industrial developments, the present governmental and nongovernmental historic preservation programs and activities are inadequate to insure future generations a genuine opportunity to appreciate and enjoy the rich heritage of our Nation."

The National Environmental Policy Act of 1969 directs the federal government to use all practical means to improve and coordinate federal programs so that important historic and cultural resources are preserved. The law requires the filing of environmental impact statements by those whose programs would affect the environment, including archaeological resources.

A Presidential Executive Order (Number 11593) spells out a policy which requires federal agencies to inventory archaeological and historical resources under their control or affected by their programs, and to exercise consideration for these resources in planning future programs.

While a few federal agencies, namely the Forest Service, the Bureau of Land Management, and the Army Corps of Engineers, have begun to employ archaeologists, the main responsibility is vested in the National Park Service of the Department of the Interior. Although the stated objectives of the laws are commendable, there is much to be desired in their implementation. The laws are comparatively new, and unknown numbers of sites most certainly have been inadvertently destroyed.

The artifact hunter should lend support to archaeologists, whose efforts to preserve information about our predecessors should be well appreciated by the public.

A list of the principal National Park Service, Washington, D.C. offices follows:

National Park Service Offices

Office of Chief Archaeologist
Division of Archaeology and Anthropology
National Park Service
Department of the Interior
Washington, D.C. 20240

Historic Preservation Team
Denver Service Center
National Park Service
7200 West Alameda Avenue
Denver, CO

Southeast Archaeological Center
National Park Service
P. O. Box 2416
Tallahassee, FL 32304

(Florida, Georgia, Alabama, Mississippi, Tennessee, Kentucky, North Carolina, South Carolina, Puerto Rico, Virgin Islands)

Midwest Archaeological Center
National Park Service
2605 North 27th Street
Lincoln, NB 68504

(Utah, Colorado, Kansas, Missouri, Iowa, Nebraska, Wyoming, South Dakota, North Dakota, Montana)

Arizona Archaeological Center
National Park Service
P. O. Box 49008
Tucson, AZ 85717

(Arizona, Nevada, California, Hawaii)

Regional Archaeologist
Northeast Region
National Park Service
143 South Third Street
Philadelphia, PA 19106

(Minnesota, Wisconsin, Michigan, Illinois, Indiana, Ohio, West Virginia, Virginia, Maryland, Delaware, Pennsylvania, New York, Connecticut, Rhode Island, Massachusetts, Vermont, New Hampshire, Maine, New Jersey)

Regional Archaeologist
Pacific Northwest Region
National Park Service
4th and Pike Building
1424 4th Avenue
Seattle, WA 98101

(Alaska, Washington, Oregon, Idaho)

Regional Archaeologist
Southwest Region
National Park Service
P.O. Box 728
Santa Fe, NM 87501

(New Mexico, Texas, Oklahoma, Arkansas, Louisiana)

National Historical Parks

Appomattox Court House, Virginia
Chalmette, Louisiana
Chesapeake & Ohio Canal, Maryland–West
    Virginia–Washington, D.C.
City of Refuge, Hawaii
Colonial, Virginia
Cumberland Gap, Kentucky–Tennessee–Virginia
George Rogers Clark, Indiana
Harpers Ferry, West Virginia–Maryland
Independence, Pennsylvania
Minute Man, Massachusetts
Morristown, New Jersey
Nez Perce, Idaho
San Juan Island, Washington
Saratoga, New York

National Monuments
Agate Fossil Beds, Nebraska
Alibates Flint Quarries and Texas Panhandle Culture, Texas
Arches, Utah

Aztec Ruins, New Mexico
Badlands, South Dakota
Bandelier, New Mexico
Biscayne, Florida
Black Canyon of the Gunnison, Colorado
Booker T. Washington, Virginia
Buck Island Reef, Virgin Islands
Cabrillo, California
Canyon de Chelly, Arizona
Capitol Reef, Utah
Capulin Mountains, New Mexico
Casa Grande Ruins, Arizona
Castillo de San Marcos, Florida
Castle Clinton, New York
Cedar Breaks, Utah
Chaco Canyon, New Mexico
Channel Islands, California
Chiricahua, Arizona
Colorado, Colorado
Craters of the Moon, Idaho
Custer Battlefield, Montana
Death Valley, California, Nevada
Devils Postpile, California
Devils Tower, Wyoming
Dinosaur, Utah, Colorado
Effigy Mounds, Iowa
El Morro, New Mexico
Florrisant Fossil Beds, Colorado
Fort Frederica, Georgia
Fort Jefferson, Florida
Fort McHenry, Maryland
Fort Matanzas, Florida
Fort Pulaski, Georgia
Fort Stanwix, New York
Fort Sumter, South Carolina
Fort Union, New Mexico
George Washington Birthplace, Virginia

George Washington Carver, Missouri
Gila Cliff Dwellings, New Mexico
Glacier Bay, Alaska
Gran Quivira, New Mexico
Grand Canyon, Arizona
Grand Portage, Minnesota
Great Sand Dunes, Colorado
Homestead, Nebraska
Hovenweek, Utah–Colorado
Jewel Cave, South Dakota
Joshua Tree, California
Katmai, Alaska
Lava Beds, California
Lehman Caves, Nevada
Marble Canyon, Arizona
Montezuma Castle, Arizona
Mound City Group, Ohio
Muir Woods, California
Natural Bridges, Utah
Navajo, Arizona
Ocmulgee, Georgia
Oregon Caves, Oregon
Organ Pipe Cactus, Arizona
Pecos, New Mexico
Perry's Victory and International Peace Memorial, Ohio
Pinnacles, California
Pipe Spring, Arizona
Pipestone, Minnesota
Rainbow Bridge, Utah
Russell Cave, Alabama
Saguaro, Arizona
Saint Croix Island, Maine
Scotts Bluff, Nebraska
Sitka, Alaska
Statue of Liberty, New York–New Jersey
Sunset Crater, Arizona
Timpanogos Cave, Utah

Tonto, Arizona
Tumacacori, Arizona
Tuzigoot, Arizona
Walnut Canyon, Arizona
White Sands, New Mexico
Wupatki, Arizona
Yucca House, Colorado

National Military Parks

Chickamauga and Chattanooga, Georgia–Tennessee
Fort Donelson, Tennessee
Fredericksburg and Spotsylvania, Virginia
Gettysburg, Pennsylvania
Guilford Courthouse, North Carolina
Horseshoe Bend, Alabama
Kings Mountain, South Carolina
Moores Creek, North Carolina
Pea Ridge, Arkansas
Shiloh, Tennessee
Vicksburg, Mississippi

National Battlefields

Big Hole, Montana
Fort Necessity, Pennsylvania
Petersburg, Virginia
Stones River, Tennessee
Tupelo, Mississippi
Wilson's Creek, Missouri

National Battlefield Parks

Kennesaw Mountain, Georgia
Manassas, Virginia
Richmond, Virginia

National Battlefield Sites

Antietam, Maryland
Brices Cross Roads, Mississippi
Cowpens, South Carolina

National Historical Sites

Abraham Lincoln Birthplace, Kentucky
Adams, Massachusetts
Allegheny Portage Railroad, Pennsylvania
Andersonville, Georgia
Andrew Johnson, Tennessee
Ansley Wilcox House, New York
Bent's Old Fort, Colorado
Carol Sandburg Home, North Carolina
Chicago Portage, Illinois
Chimney Rock, Nebraska
Christiansted, Virgin Islands
Dorchester Heights, Massachusetts
Edison, New Jersey
Eisenhower, Pennsylvania
Ford's Theatre, Washington, D.C.
Fort Bowie, Arizona
Fort Davis, Texas
Fort Laramie, Wyoming
Fort Larned, Kansas
Fort Point, California
Fort Raleigh, North Carolina
Fort Scott, Kansas
Fort Smith, Arkansas
Fort Union Trading Post, North Dakota–Montana
Fort Vancouver, Washington
Gloria Dei Church, Pennsylvania
Golden Spike, Utah
Hampton, Maryland
Herbert Hoover, Iowa

Home of Franklin D. Roosevelt, New York
Hopewell Village, Pennsylvania
Hubbell Trading Post, Arizona
Jamestown, Virgina
Jefferson National Expansion Memorial, Missouri
John Fitzgerald Kennedy, Massachusetts
John Muir, California
Lincoln Home, Illinois
Lyndon B. Johnson, Texas
McLoughlin House, Oregon
Pennsylvania Avenue, Washington, D.C.
Sagamore Hill, New York
Saint Paul's Church, New York
Saint Thomas, Virgin Islands
Saint-Gaudens, New Hampshire
Salem Maritime, Massachusetts
San Jose Mission, Texas
San Juan, Puerto Rico
Saugus Iron Works, Massachusetts
The Mar-A-Lago, Florida
Theodore Roosevelt Birthplace, New York
Touro Synagogue, Rhode Island
Vanderbilt Mansion, New York
Whitman Mission, Washington
William Howard Taft, Ohio

National Memorials

Arkansas Post, Arkansas
Chamizal, Texas
Coronado, Arizona
Custis–Lee Mansion, Virginia
DeSoto, Florida
Federal Hall, New York
Fort Caroline, Florida
Fort Clatsop, Oregon
Frederick Douglass Home, Washington, D.C.

General Grant, New York
Hamilton Grange, New York
Johnstown Flood, Pennsylvania
Lincoln Boyhood, Indiana
Lincoln Memorial, Washington, D.C.
Mount Rushmore, South Dakota
Roger Williams, Rhode Island
Thomas Jefferson, Washington, D.C.
Washington Monument, Washington, D.C
Wright Brothers, North Carolina

National Cemeteries

Antietam, Maryland
Battleground, Washington, D.C.
Fort Donelson, Tennessee
Fredericksburg, Virginia
Gettysburg, Pennsylvania
Poplar Grove, Virginia
Shiloh, Tennessee
Stones River, Tennessee
Vicksburg, Mississippi
Yorktown, Virginia

National Parks

Acadia, Maine
Big Bend, Texas
Bryce Canyon, Utah
Canyonlands, Utah
Carlsbad Caverns, New Mexico
Crater Lake, Oregon
Everglades, Florida
Glacier, Montana
Grand Canyon, Arizona
Grand Teton, Wyoming
Great Smoky Mountains, Tennessee–North Carolina

Guadalupe Mountains, Texas
Haleakala, Hawaii
Hawaii Volcanoes, Hawaii
Hot Springs, Arkansas
Isle Royale, Michigan
Kings Canyon, California
Lassen Volcanic, California
Mammoth Cave, Kentucky
Mesa Verde, Colorado
Mount McKinley, Alaska
Mount Rainier, Washington
North Cascades, Washington
Olympic, Washington
Petrified Forest, Arizona
Platt, Oklahoma
Redwood, California
Rocky Mountian, Colorado
Sequoia, California
Shenandoah, Virginia
Virgin Islands, Virgin Islands
Voyageurs, Minnesota
Wind Cave, South Dakota
Yellowstone, Wyoming–Montana–Idaho
Yosemite, California
Zion, Utah

Appendix B

State-by-State Listing of Archaeologists and Publications

MOST (but not all) states have legislation affecting archaeological resources. In general these laws regulate disturbances of archaeological resources on state land and, in some instances and to different degrees, on private land.

These laws vary considerably from state to state; local inquiry is necessary. One source which reviews all state programs and which cites both state and federal legislation affecting archaeological resources (as of 1971) is *Public Archaeology* by Charles R. McGimsey III, available from Seminar Press, 111 Fifth Avenue, New York City, NY.

I wrote to the governors of all fifty states asking for the name and address of the state archaeologist and for names of publications on the archaeology and archaeological organizations of the

---

The spelling of the word archaeology (archeology) will appear throughout this chapter in both forms (with and without the letter *a*). I have used the word as it is spelled by the individuals and organizations. It is spelled both ways by respected authorities in the field.

state. The objective was to supply the reader sources of information on the archaeology of his or her state.

The state-by-state list as supplied by the governors or their staffs along with information obtained from the Society For American Archeology, 1703 New Hampshire Avenue, N.W., Washington D.C., follows:

Alabama

There is no one person designated as the state archaeologist in Alabama, but there are archaeologists on the staff of the Alabama Historical Commission. The address is:

> Alabama Historical Commission
> Rice–Semple–Haardt House
> 725 Monroe Street
> Montgomery, AL

There are departments of archaeology at the University of Alabama in Birmingham, Auburn University in Montgomery, and the University of South Alabama in Mobile.

There is a museum at the University of Alabama, Tuscaloosa, AL 35401.

The Alabama Archaeological Society publishes a journal. Its addresses are:

> Amos J. Wright
> Alabama Archaeological Society
> 2602 Green Mountain Road, S.E.
> Huntsville, AL 35803

> David L. DeJarnette, Editor
> *Journal of the Alabama Archaeological Society*
> Box 307
> Orange Beach, AL 36561

Alaska

Alaska's state archaeologist is:

Douglas Reger
Office of History and Archaeology
Alaska Division of Parks
Suite 210
619 Warehouse Drive
Anchorage, AK 99501

While there is no state archaeological society, there is an organization called the Alaska Anthropological Association. The current president is:

Dr. William B. Workman
Alaska Anthropological Association
University of Alaska
3221 Providence Drive
Anchorage, AK 99504

There are innumerable publications dealing with archaeology in Alaska, including professional journals and published books.

Two books of general interest on the archaeology of Alaska are recommended: *Ancient Men in the Arctic* by J.L. Giddings, published by Alfred A. Knopf in New York; and *The Eskimos and Aleuts* by Don E. Dumond, published by Thames and Hudson. There are two museums:

Alaska Historical Library and Museum
P.O. Box 2051
Juneau, AK 99801

University of Alaska Museum
College, AK 99701

Arizona

There is no state archaeologist for Arizona.

A quarterly, titled *Kiva* (subscription price per volume $10) is published by:

> The Arizona Archaeological and Historical Society
> Arizona State Museum
> University of Arizona
> North Park Avenue at 3rd Street
> Tucson, AZ 85721

A subscription to *Plateau* is obtained by joining the Northern Arizona Museum for $25.

> Northern Arizona Museum
> Route 4, Box 720
> Flagstaff, AZ 86001

Arkansas

> Hester Davis
> State Archaeologist
> Arkansas Archaeological Survey
> University of Arkansas
> Fayetteville, AR 72701

> University of Arkansas Museum
> University Hall
> Fayetteville, AR 72701

California

> Francis Riddell
> Senior Archaelogist
> Department of Parks and Recreation
> Box 2390
> Sacramento, CA 95811

Robert H. Lowie Museum
2620 Bancroft Way
University of California
Berkeley, CA

Southwest Museum
10 Highland Park
Los Angeles, CA 90042

Archaeological Survey Association of Southern California
Southwest Museum
Los Angeles, CA 90042

Central California Archaeological Foundation
Sacramento State College
Sacramento, CA 95819

California State Indian Museum
2618 K Street
Sacramento, CA

San Diego Museum of Man
Balboa Park
San Diego, CA

Society for California Archeology
Business Office
Anthropology Department
California State University
Fullerton, CA 92634

Colorado

Bruce E. Rippeteau
State Archaeologist
1300 Broadway
Denver, CO 80203

Colorado Archaeological Society
University of Colorado
Boulder, CO 80302

University of Colorado Museum
Broadway between 15th and 16th Streets
Boulder, CO 80904

Connecticut

The state archaeologist of Connecticut is:

Professor Douglas F. Jordan
University of Connecticut
Storrs, CT 06268

The Archaeological Society of Connecticut, Inc., may be reached:

c/o Department of Archaeology
Central Connecticut State College
1615 Stanley Street
New Britain, CT 06050

Delaware

Delaware now has four archaeologists working with the Division of Historical and Cultural Affairs, Bureau of Archaeology and Historic Preservation. They may be reached through:

Daniel R. Griffith
Archaeologist
Bureau of Archaeology and Historic Preservation
Hall of Records
P.O. Box 1401
Dover, DE 19901

There are two archaeological societies in Delaware and one regional conference of professional archaeologists who work in the Mid-Atlantic area:

The Archeological Society of Delaware
c/o Martha Schiek
101 Myrtle Avenue
Claymont, DE 19703

The Sussex Society of Archeology & History
c/o Elizabeth Higgins
512 Poplar Street
Seaford, DE 19973

The Mid-Atlantic Archeological Conference
c/o Dr. William Gardner
Department of Anthropology
The Catholic University of America
Washington, D.C. 20017

A number of publications may be ordered from:

Richard Artusy
Island Field Museum
R.D. #2
Box 126
Milford, DE 19963

They are:

"A Brief Account of the Indians of Delaware" (50¢)
"Brief Survey of Prehistoric Man on the Delmarva Penin-
    sula" (45¢)
"Coloring Book of the First Americans, Lenape Drawings"
    ($1.95)
"Handbook for Delmarva Archaeology" ($2.50)
"Hunters and Fishermen of Prehistoric Delaware" (30¢)

"Island Field: A Prehistoric Village and Cemetary" (35¢)
"Middle Woodland Cemetery in Central Delaware: Excavations at the Island Field Site" ($1.50)
"Middle Woodland Ceramics from Wolfe Neck, Sussex County and Delaware" (2.25)
"Prehistory of Delaware" (10¢)

Florida

L. Ross Morrell
State Archaeologist
Division of Archives, History and Records Management
The Capitol
Tallahassee, FL 32304

The state archaeological society in Florida is:

Florida Anthropological Society
Dr. Raymond Williams, President
Department of Anthropology
University of South Florida
Tampa, FL

The society publishes a journal, *The Florida Anthropologist*. For information and a subscription write:

Dr. Jerald T. Milanich
Division of Social Services
Florida State Museum
Gainesville, FL 32601

Florida State University Museum
Dogwood Way
Tallahassee, FL 32306

Georgia

Lewis H. Larson, Jr.
State Archaeologist
West Georgia College
103 Martha Munro Hall
Carrollton, GA 30118

The state archaeological organization is the Society for Georgia Archaeology. The regular membership dues are $6. This entitles you to receive a copy of *Early Georgia*, a scholarly journal of Southeastern archaeology and the "Profile," the quarterly newsletter of the Society. Write to:

Frankie Snow
Treasurer
Society for Georgia Archaaology
209 N. Grady Avenue
Douglas, GA 31533

Two publications on the archaeology of Georgia are *Anthropological Papers of the University of Georgia* and the *Laboratory of Archaeological Reports*. Information on these publications may be obtained from the:

University of Georgia
Department of Anthropology
Athens, GA 30602

An excellent booklet with considerable information is the "Historic Preservation Handbook" prepared by the:

Historic Preservation Section
Department of Natural Resources
270 Washington Street, S.W.
Atlanta, GA 30334

The address of the Northwest Georgia Archaeological Society is:

Northwest Georgia Archaeological Society
Shorter College
Rome, GA 30161

Hawaii

Hawaii does not have a position of state archaeologist. However, Dr. Robert J. Hommon, an archaeologist, handles the archaeological program within the historic sites section of the Division of State Parks. His address is:

Dr. Robert J. Hommon
Division of State Parks
Outdoor Recreation and Historic Sites
Department of Land and Natural Resources
P.O. Box 621
Honolulu, HI 96809

There is no state professional organization in the field of archaeology.

A list of publications in the field of archaeology can be obtained from:

Bishop Museum
P.O. Box 6037
Honolulu, HI 96818

University of Hawaii Press
2840 Kolowalu Street
Honolulu, HI 96822

Archaeological Research Center Hawaii
P.O. Box 285
Lawai, HI 96765

There is a museum:

Bernice P. Bishop Museum
1355 Kalihi Street
Honolulu, HI 96819

Idaho

Thomas J. Green is the state archaeologist for Idaho. His address is:

Thomas J. Green
Idaho State Historical Society
610 North Julia Davis Drive
Boise, ID 83706

There. is an amateur society called the Idaho Archaeological Society:

Mr. John Schaertl, President
6614 Hummel Drive
Boise, ID 83706

There is also a regional professional society:

Northwest Anthropological Conference
Department of Anthropology
Washington State University
Pullman, WA 99164

There are several publications dealing with Idaho archaeology.

Tebiwa
The Journal of the Idaho State University Museum
Idaho State University
Pocatello, ID 83209

Occasional Papers of the Museum
Idaho State University Museum
Idaho State University
Pocatello, ID 83209

*University of Idaho Anthropological Research Manuscript
Series*
Laboratory of Anthropology
University of Idaho
Moscow, ID 83843

Northwest Anthropological Research Notes
Department of Anthropology
University of Idaho
Moscow, ID 83843

Illinois

Illinois State Archaeological Society
Southern Illinois University Museum
Carbondale, IL 62901

The Illinois State Museum has a list of publications that deal
with archaeology.

The Illinois State Museum
Spring and Edwards Street
Springfield, IL 62607

"Preliminary Report of 1972 Historic Sites Survey Archaeological Reconnaissance of Selected Areas in the State of Illinois."

Illinois Archaeological Survey
109 Davenport Hall
University of Illinois
Urbana, IL

A quarterly newsletter is published by

Illinois Association for Advancement of Archaeology
Eugene M. Gray, Editor
102 Circle Drive
Cambridge, IL 61238

The Central States Archaeological Societies, Inc., includes societies in Illinois, Indiana, Missouri, northwest Arkansas, Kentucky, Tennessee, Iowa, Wisconsin, and Georgia. They publish the *Central States Archaeological Journal.*

> Mr. Dale Van Blair, Editor
> 17 Birch Drive
> Belleville, IL 62223

Indiana

Governor Otis R. Bowen has just appointed the first archaeologist for the state of Indiana. He is Gary D. Ellis, who will work out of a new section, the Division of Historic Preservation, within the Department of Natural Resources.

> Gary D. Ellis
> Division of Historic Preservation
> Department of Natural Resources
> Indiana State Museum
> 202 N. Alabama
> Indianapolis, Indiana 46204

The *Sunday Section* of the February 5, 1978, issue of the *Indianapolis Sunday Star* is devoted to the archaeology of Indiana.

The Wabash Valley Archaeological Society offers each summer a three-day adult field workshop for professionals, university students, and amateur archaeologists.

Iowa

The office of the state archaeologist for Iowa is the:

> East Lawn Building
> Iowa City, IA

It is staffed by Duane C. Anderson, director; John Hotopp, surveys; Julianne Hoyer, editor of publications; Marshel McKusick, research archaeologist; and Richard Slattery, field representative.

Iowa Archaeological Society
State University of Iowa
Museum of Natural History
Iowa City, IA 52240

Kansas

The state archaeologist of Kansas is:

Mr. Thomas A. Witty
Kansas Historical Society
120 West 10th Street
Topeka, KS 66612

Kansas Anthropological Society
c/o Kansas State Historical Society
120 West 10th Street
Topeka, KS 66612

Kentucky

The state archaeologist for Kentucky is:

Dr. Berle Clay
Department of Anthropology
Lafferty Hall
University of Kentucky
Lexington, KY 40506

There are two archaeological societies:

The W.S. Webb Archaeological Society
(Headquarters—same address as Dr. Clay)

Kentucky Archaeological Association
Mr. Vernon White, Treasurer
Department of Sociology and Anthropology
Western Kentucky University
Bowling Green, KY 42101

"A Bibliography of Kentucky Archaeology" by Mary Bowman, published in 1973, priced at $3, is available from Vernon White at above address. Dr. Clay is working on an update of the bibliography.

The Kentucky Heritage Commission has published various county studies on the archaeology of Kentucky which are available for $5 each.

Mrs. Eldred Melton
Executive Director
Kentucky Heritage Commission
104 Bridge Street
Frankfort, KY 40601

Museum of Anthropology
University of Kentucky
Lexington, KY 40506

Louisiana

The state archaeologist of Louisiana is:

Dr. Alan Toth
P. O. Box 44247
Baton Rouge, LA 70804

His office is in the Louisiana Department of Culture, Recreation and Tourism, under Mr. Paul B. Hartwig, director of Archaeology and Historic Preservation. This department at address given publishes a popular series in archaeology that is distributed free.

The Louisiana Archaeological Society publishes a quarterly newsletter and an annual bulletin for its members. The dues are $10 per year.

Dr. Jon L. Gibson, Editor
120 Beta Drive
Lafayette, LA 70506

"A Bibliography Relative to Indians of the State of Louisiana" is published by the Louisiana Geological Survey.

Louisiana Geological Survey
Department of Natural Resources
Box G
Baton Rouge, LA 70893

Dan Shipman, President
Louisiana Archaeological Society
926 Webster Street
New Orleans, LA 70118

Joseph B. Toups
Imperial Calcasieu Chapter
Louisiana Archaeological Society
920 11th Street
Lake Charles, LA 70601

Forrest Travirca
Delta Chapter
Louisiana Archaeological Society
P.O. Box 181
Lockport, LA 70374

Lynn Sibley
East Central Chapter
Louisiana Archaeological Society
1907 Shannon Road
Alexandria, LA 71301

Lester Davis
Northeast Chapter
Louisiana Archaeological Society
816 Rymes Circle
Monroe, LA 71201

Bill Bourne
Baton Rouge Chapter
Louisiana Archaeological Society
9737 N. Winston Street
Baton Rouge, LA 70809

Maine

Maine does not have a state archaeologist; however, serving in a comparable capacity is:

Dr. Bruce J. Bourque
Research Associate for Archaeology
Maine State Museum
State House
Augusta, ME 04330

The Maine Historic Preservation Commission will be engaging an archaeologist to assist in checking proposed construction sites for archaeological importance.
There is a state amateur society:

Maine Archaeological Society
c/o Robert McKay
Department of Anthropology
University of Maine
Orono, ME 04473

The comprehensive list of publications on Maine archaeology is lengthy. References to these are cited in recent articles, by B. Bourque, D. Sanger, and D. Snow in the journal *Arctic Anthropology*, Volume 12, Number 2, 1975; a series of articles by Bourque, Sanger, Snow and others in a journal titled, *Man in the Northeast*.

Robert Abbe Museum of Stone Age Antiquities
Bar Harbor, ME 04609

Maryland

The Maryland state archaeologist is:

Tyler Bastian
Maryland Geological Survey
Merryman Hall
Johns Hopkins University
Baltimore, MD 21218

There is an active state archaeological society with ten local chapters:

Archaeological Society of Maryland, Inc.
729 Hollen Road
Baltimore, MD 21212

The ten local chapters are:

Anne Arundel County Archeological Society
Baltimore County Archeological Society
Catonsville Archeological Society
Central (Baltimore City area)
Harford County
Lower Delmarva (Somerset, Wicomico, Worcester counties)
Mid-Shore (Caroline, Dorchester, Queen Annes, Talbot counties)
Northeastern (northern Eastern Shore)
Pikesville–Milford (northwest suburban Baltimore high schools)
Southwestern (Washington, D.C., and Maryland suburbs)

The society provides opportunities for public participation in local archaeological activities. Membership is $5 per year.

The society publishes a biannual journal, *Maryland Archaeology*, and a monthly newsletter. There is a lengthy list of publications on Maryland archaeology. These may be ordered from:

Paul Cresthull
Editor
Maryland Archaeology
721 Hookers Mill Road
Abingdon, MD 21009

The regional archaeological organization is:

Middle Atlantic Archeological Conference
Department of Anthropology
Catholic University of America
Washington, D.C. 20017

Massachusetts

The Massachusetts Historical Commission employs an archaeologist:

Valery Talmadge
294 Washington Street
Boston, MA

The state historian is:

Dr. Maurice Robbins
Bronson Museum
8 North Main Street
Attleboro, MA 02703

Governor Michael Dukakis advises me that these individuals can supply information on the publications related to archaeology in Massachusetts.

Massachusetts Archeological Society
Bronson Museum
8 North Main Street
Attleboro, MA 02703

Michigan

John R. Halsey
State Archaeologist
Michigan History Division
208 N. Capitol Avenue
Lansing, MI 48918

Michigan Archeological Society
c/o Museum of Anthropology
University of Michigan
Ann Arbor, MI 48104

The Michigan Archaeological Society has nine local chapters with both professional and amateur members. The dues are $6 and members receive a quarterly publication, *Michigan Archaeologist*, edited by Dr. James E. Fitting.

Dr. James E. Fitting, Editor
Michigan Archaeologist
237 Kedzie
East Lansing, MI 48823

The Archaeology of Michigan by Dr. James E. Fitting, published by Cranbrook Institute of Science ($5.95), chronicles archaeological excavations of the past decade and a half.

Cranbrook Institute of Science
P.O. Box 807
Bloomfield Hills, MI 48013.

A number of monographs on Michigan archaeological sites have been published by the University of Michigan, Museum of Anthropology, Ann Arbor, Michigan 48109.

Minnesota

The Minnesota state archaeologist is:

Elden Johnson
215 Ford Hall
224 Church Street, S. E.
Minneapolis, MN 55455

Minnesota Archaeological Society
Building 27
Ft. Snelling
St. Paul, MN 55111

The Minnesota Archaeological Society publishes a quarterly journal, *Minnesota Archaeologist.* Cost is $4 per year.

Minnesota Historical Society
1500 Mississippi Street
St. Paul, MN 55101

This society has published a number of books. (When ordering these add 50¢ for postage.) *Burial Mounds of Central Minnesota—Excavation Reports* ($3.25), *The Prehistoric Peoples of Minnesota* ($1.50), *Roster of Excavated Prehistoric Sites in Minnesota* ($2.50), *Burial Mounds of the Red River Headwaters* ($2.00), *Voices From the Rapids—An Underwater Search for Fur Trade Artifacts* ($6.50). A list of others is also available.

Mississippi

While there is no officially designated state archaeologist for Mississippi, Sam McGahey is currently serving in that capacity:

Sam McGahey
Archaeologist
Department of Archives and History
P. O. Box 571
Jackson, MS 39205

There is a Mississippi Archaeological Association. For information write to:

Mrs. Mary Neumaier
115 Wiltshire Boulevard
Biloxi, MS 39531

The association publishes *Mississippi Archaeology*, edited by Mr. McGahey, 10 times a year. It is mailed to associate members. Dues are $5 for active members. Letters regarding membership should be addressed to:

Mississippi Archaeological Association
P.O. Box 23
Leland, MS 38756

Mississippi Department of Archives and History
P.O. Box 571
Jackson, MS 39205

The Department of Archives has a number of publications, some of which are: *Archaeological Survey in Mississippi* ($5.80), *Archaeological Excavation at the Boyd Site, Tunica County* ($4.45), *Archaeological Survey in the Tombigbee River Drainage Area* ($2.35); *Archaeology of the Fatherland Site—The Grand Village of the Natchez* ($4.45).

There is a complete bibliography, "Mississippi Archaeology," of some twenty pages compiled by Brent W. Smith, that includes material on other areas of the Mississippi River drainage area.

Mississippi State Historical Museum
Capitol and N. State Streets
Jackson, MS 39505

Missouri

Missouri's archaeologist is:

Michael Weichman
Office of Historic Preservation
Department of Natural Resources
P.O. Box 176
Jefferson City, MO 65101

Missouri Archaeological Society
P.O. Box 958
15 Switzler Hall
University of Missouri
Columbia MO 65201

Membership cost in the society is $7.50 per year. This entitles members to ten issues of the newsletter per year and one volume of *The Missouri Archaeologist.* The society also has a six-page bibliography of publications detailing Missouri archaeology, which are available for purchase.

Montana

Montana Archaeological Society
Montana State University Museum
Missoula, MT 59801

Nebraska

Although Nebraska does not have a designated state archaeologist, there is a professional archaeologist, and his staff includes eight archaeologists:

Marvin F. Kivett
Director
Nebraska State Historical Society
1500 R Street
Lincoln, NB 68508

There are eight archaeologists on the staff of:

The Department of Anthropology
University of Nebraska
Lincoln, NB

The Nebraska State Historical Society has a bibliography of publications on prehistory, archaeology, and Indians related to Nebraska.
Prehistoric Man on the Great Plains by Dr. Waldo R. Wedel was published by the University of Oklahoma Press ($6.95).

University of Nebraska State Museum
101 Morrill Hall
14th and U Streets
Lincoln, NB 68508

Nevada

Nevada has three archaeologists whose combined duties might be considered the equivalent of a state archaeologist:

Donald R. Tuohy
Curator of Anthropology
Nevada State Museum
Capitol Complex
Carson City, NV 89710

Hal Turner
Roadside Development and Environmental Services
Department of Highways
State of Nevada
Carson City, NV 89712

Charles Zeier
Department of Historic Preservation and Archeology
Division of Conservation and Natural Resources
201 South Fall Street
Capitol Complex
Carson City, NV 89710

There are two amateur archaeological organizations:

Archaeo-Nevada Society
P.O. Box 5744
Las Vegas, NV 89102

Am-Arcs of Nevada
Nevada Archaeological Society
University of Nevada
Reno, NV 89507

The Nevada State Museum at Carson City has publications for sale, among which are *Archaeological Survey in Southwestern Idaho and Northern Nevada,* by Donald R. Tuohy ($3.50), and *Miscellaneous Papers on Nevada Archaeology* ($4.95).

New Hampshire

The state archaeologist for New Hampshire is:

Dr. Gary Hume
University of New Hampshire
Durham, NH 03824

Also contact:

Professor Charles Bolian
Department of Anthropology
University of New Hampshire
Horton Center
Durham, NH 03824

Eugene Winter
President
New Hampshire Society of Archaeologists
54 Trull Lane
Lowell, MA 01852

Marjorie Chandler
Secretary
New Hampsire Society of Archaeologists
Averill Road
Brookline, NH

The society publishes a bulletin edited by:

Paul E. Holmes
Star Route
Plaistow, NH 03865

New Jersey

The state archaeologist for New Jersey is:

Dr. Lorraine E. Williams
Bureau of Archaeology and Ethnology
New Jersey State Museum
Trenton, NJ 08625

Archeological Society of New Jersey
New Jersey State Museum
West State Street
Trenton, NJ 18625

The society has another office:

c/o Professor Herbert Kraft
Seton Hall University
South Orange, NJ

There are a number of publications dealing with various aspects of archaeology in New Jersey. Among these are: "Indian Habitation in Sussex County, New Jersey," Bulletin 13 Geological Survey of New Jersey, Trenton; "Excavations at the Zipser Lower Field Site," by Lorraine E. Williams, Bulletin No. 28:16-18, Archaeological Society of New Jersey; "Archaeology of the Tocks Island Area," by Herbert Kraft, Seton Hall University Press.

New Mexico

The state archaeologist for New Mexico is:

Stewart L. Peckham
Curator of the Laboratory of Anthropology
Museum of New Mexico
P.O. Box 2087
Santa Fe, NM 87503

During the past twenty-five years, the Museum of New Mexico has excavated more than four hundred prehistoric and historic sites. Peckham is planning a series of publications which will deal with the archaeology of the state area by area.

There are two books that include archaeology of New Mexico: *An Introduction to the Study of Southwestern Archaeology*, by Alfred Vincent Kidder, Yale University Press ($3.95), and *Prehistoric Indians of the Southwest*, by H.M. Wormington, Denver Museum of Natural History.

Archaeological Society of New Mexico
P.O. Box 3485
Albuquerque, NM 87110

This society is one of the oldest in the nation. It has twelve affiliated chapters:

Albuquerque Archaeological Society
P.O. Box 4029
Albuquerque, NM 87106

Dona Ana Archaeological Society
2057 Avalon
Las Cruces, NM 88001

El Paso Archaeological Society, Inc.
P.O. Box 4345
El Paso, TX 79914

Friends of Raton Anthropology
Arthur Johnson Memorial Library
Raton, NM 87740

Gallup Archaeological Society
Box 131
Gallup, NM 87301

Grant County Archaeological Society
Mrs. Aggie Haymes, President
307 East 19th Street
Silver City, NM 88061

Lea County Archaeological Society
P.O. Box 1363
Hobbs, NM 88240

Los Alamos Archaeological Society
c/o Anne V. Poore, President
111 Andanada
Los Alamos, NM 87544

Plateau Sciences Society
c/o Red Rock State Park
P.O. Box 328
Church Rock, NM 87311

San Juan Country Archaeological Society
P.O. Box 970
Aztec, NM 87410

San Juan Museum Association
Route 3, Box 169
Farmington, NM 87401

New York

Dr. Robert Funk
State Archaeologist
New York State Museum
Albany, NY 12222

New York Archaeological Association
Rochester Museum and Science Center
657 East Avenue
Rochester, NY 14607

North Carolina

The North Carolina state archaeologist is:

Ms. Jacqueline R. Fehon
Archeology Branch
Dept. of Cultural Resources
109 E. Jones Street
Raleigh, NC 27611

In addition, the Archaeology Branch has a staff of six full-time archaeologists.

There is a separate underwater archaeology unit which was mentioned in an earlier chapter of this book:

Gordon P. Watts, Jr.
Director
Underwater Archeological Research Unit
Fort Fisher
Box 58
Kure Beach, NC 28449

The archaeological society publishes a journal, *Southern Indian Studies*, and a newsletter, both of which are available to society members.

Tucker R. Littleton
President
North Carolina Archeological Society
P.O. Box 488
Swansborough, NC 28584

There is a professional organization of archaeologists in the state called the North Carolina Archeological Council.

The Council and the Archaeology Branch, Division of Archives and History, Department of Cultural Resources have compiled a comprehensive bibliography, "Anthropological Bibliography of North Carolina." This listing and another, "Publications of the Division of Archives and History," are available from the:

Historical Publications Section
Division of Archives and History
North Carolina Department of Cultural Resources
109 East Jones Street
Raleigh, NC 27611

North Dakota

The state archaeologist of North Dakota is:

Nick G. Franke
Research Archeologist
State Historical Society of North Dakota
Liberty Memorial Building
Capitol Grounds
Bismarck, ND 58505

There is no state archaeological society. The Plains Conference is a regional organization of professional archaeologists studying the archaeology of the plains.

Plains Conference
Department of Anthropology
Colorado State University
Fort Collins, CO 80523

While there are a large number of publications about archaeology in North Dakota, most of them are journal articles or out of print publications.

State Historical Society Museum
Liberty Memorial Building
Bismarck, ND 58501

Ohio

Martha Potter Otto
Curator of Archaeology
Ohio Historical Center
1813 N. High Street
Columbus, OH 43210

Cleveland Natural Science Museum
10600 East Boulevard
Cleveland, OH 44106

Oklahoma

Oklahoma's state archaeologist is:

Dr. Don G. Wyckoff
University of Oklahoma
1335 South Asp
Norman, OK 73109

The Archaeological Survey publishes a series which is available on request. The address is the same as Dr. Wyckoff's.

The Oklahoma Archaeological Society, composed of professionals and amateurs, publishes nine issues of a monthly newsletter. The subscription cost is $7.50.

The correspondence secretary of the Oklahoma Archaeological Society is:

Ms. Dorothy Phillips
2217 Arlington Drive
Oklahoma City, OK 73108

J. Willis Stavall Museum of Science and History
1335 South Asp Street
Norman, OK 73109

Oregon

Oregon Archaeological Society
P.O. Box 13293
Portland, OR 97213

Museum of Natural History
University of Oregon
Eugene, OR 97403

The museum issued a bibliography in 1969.

Pennsylvania

Pennsylvania's state archaeologist is:

Dr. Barry C. Kent
Pennsylvania Historical and Museum Commission
P.O. Box 1026
Harrisburg, PA 17120

Pennsylvania has a program to register Indian sites. Should you discover a site you feel to be of importance, you may write for a site survey form. If it appears to be an important site, the Archaeology Section will assign a site number which will identify it permanently. They promise to keep the information confidential.

Those in the eastern part of Pennsylvania may write to the:

Archaeology Section
William Penn Memorial Museum
Harrisburg, PA 17108

Those in the western part of the state should write to:

Section of Man
Carnegie Museum
Pittsburgh, PA 15213

The Society for Pennsylvania Archaeology, Inc., publishes a quarterly bulletin, *Pennsylvania Archaeologist*. Membership dues are $6. Make checks payable to Treasurer, SPA, and mail to:

Roger W. Moeller
Treasurer
American Indian Archaeological Institute
Box 85
Washington, CT 06793

"The Society was organized in 1929 to promote the study of the archaeology of Pennsylvania and of the neighboring states; to encourage scientific research and excavation and to discourage unscientific exploration, that is, without proper recording and cataloging; to promote the conservation of archaeological sites and artifacts through legislation and education; to oppose the manufacture and the sale of fraudulent antiquities; to encourage the establishment of local archaeological museums and societies; to promote the dissemination of archaeological knowledge by means of publications and forums; and to encourage and foster the exchange of knowledge between professional and non-professional archaeologists."

The Pennsylvania Historical and Museum Commission has published a "Book and Publication List, 1977-78" that includes a number of items dealing with Pennsylvania archaeology. Recommended is *Foundations of Pennsylvania Archaeology* ($10).

Rhode Island

While Rhode Island has no state archaeologist by title, The Rhode Island Historical Preservation Commission serves in this capacity. They have two full-time staff archaeologists:

John Senulis and Gail Brown
150 Benefit Street
Providence, RI 02903

Narragansett Archaeological Society of Rhode Island
277 Brook Street
Providence, RI 20906

South Carolina

The state archaeologist of South Carolina is:

Robert L. Stephenson
Director
Institute of Archeology and Anthropology
University of South Carolina
Columbia, SC 29208

The institute sponsors the archaeological society of South Carolina with above mailing address. Membership dues are $6, and three regularly issued publications are available to members: "Features & Profiles," a six to eight-page monthly newsletter; *South Carolina Antiquities,* a journal published twice annually; and *The Notebook,* a bi-monthly journal of the Institute available to Society members free upon request.

The Institute of Archeology and Anthropology has an active publishing program on its research; namely, Anthropological Studies and Research Manuscript Series.

Two recent publications are *Palmetto Parapets* by Stanley South ($5) and *Camden, A Frontier Town* by Kenneth E. Lewis ($7.95).

South Dakota

The state archaeologist of South Dakota is:

Robert Alex
P.O. Box 152
Fort Meade, SD

South Dakota Archeological
c/o South Dakota Museum
University of South Carolina
Vermillion, SD 57069

Tennessee

The state archaeologist of Tennessee is:

Joseph L. Benthall
Director of the Division of Archaeology
Department of Conservation
5103 Edmondson Pike
Nashville, TN 37211

There are three major archaeological societies within the state:

Tennessee Archaeological Society
c/o Orlenas L. Rice, Jr.
President
308 East Forest Road
Oak Ridge, TN 37830

Tennessee Anthropological Association
c/o Dr. Charles H. Faulkner
Department of Anthropology
South Stadium Hall
University of Tennessee
Knoxville, TN 37901

Volunteer State Archaeological Society of Tennessee
c/o Bobby Hendricks
President
114 Savely Court
Hendersonville, TN 37075

There are a large number of publications on archaeology in Tennessee. You may obtain a list from the:

University of Tennessee Press
University of Tennessee
Knoxville, TN

Another list was prepared in the Tennessee Valley Authority. Write to:

Dr. Major C. R. McCullough
Mapping Services Branch
Tennessee Valley Authority
200 Haney Building
Chattanooga TN 37401

The Division of Archaeology has begun a publication series with *An Archaeological and Historical Assessment of the First Hermitage, 1976* by Samuel D. Smith ($5.45).

The Tennessee Anthropological Association has a published list of references, "A Bibliography of Tennessee Anthropology, including Cherokee, Chickasaw, and McLungeon Studies."

Frank McLung Museum
1027 Circle Park S.W.
Knoxville, TN 37916

Texas

Curtis Tunnell
State Archaeologist
Box 12276 Capitol Station
Austin, TX 73711

Midland Archaeological Society
P. O. Box 4224
Midland, TX 79701

Texas Archeological Society
c/o Department of Anthropology
University of Texas
Austin, TX

Utah

The state archaeologist for Utah is:

Dr. David B. Madsen
Director
State Antiquities Section of the
    Division of State History
603 East South Temple
Salt Lake City, UT 84102

There are a number of professional and amateur archaeological organizations in the state.

Utah Statewide Archeological Society
4283 Bennion
Salt Lake City, UT 84119

Utah Archeological Research Council
603 East South Temple
Salt Lake City, UT 84102

Antiquities Committee
603 East South Temple
Salt Lake City, UT 84102

There are more than five hundred publications on the prehistory of Utah. A general up-to-date overview is the *Prehistory of Utah and the Eastern Great Basin: A Review 1968-1976* ($8) from the University of Utah Press.

Anthropology Museum
University of Utah
Building 411
Salt Lake City, UT 84112

Vermont

The state archaeologist of Vermont is:

Ms. Giovanna Neudorfer
Division for Historic Preservation
Pavilion Building
Montpelier, VT 05602

The official state society is the:

Vermont Archeological Society
Box 663
Burlington, VT 05401

The membership is $5 for which you also receive four newsletters a year.

There are numerous papers on Vermont archaeology in various journals. *Archeology in Vermont* by John C. Huden ($3.50) may be purchased from the:

Vermont Historical Society
Pavilion Building
Montpelier, VT 05602

Vermont Historical Society
State Administration Building
State Street
Montpelier, VT 05602

Virginia

The state archaeologist for Virginia is:

Dr. William Kelso
Commissioner of Archaeology
Wrenn Building
College of William and Mary
Williamsburg, VA 23185

Virginia State Library
Richmond, VA 23225

The Chesopiean Archaeological Association publishes a bimonthly *The Chesopiean: A Journal of North American Archaeology*. It is most readable, informative, and illustrated and worth the subscription of $7.50 per year.

Floyd Painter, Editor
The Chesopiean
7507 Pennington Road
Norfolk, VA

Washington

Washington Archeological Society
Box 84
University Station
Seattle, WA 98105

West Virginia

Daniel Fowler
Archaeological Administrator
Geological and Economic Survey
P.O. Box 879
Morgantown, WV 26505

Earl R. Walter
President
West Virginia Archeological Society
821 Spring Road
Charleston, WV 25314

Wisconsin

The state archaeologist for Wisconsin is:

Dr. Joan E. Freeman
State Historical Society of Wisconsin Museum
816 State Street
Madison, WI 53706

The state amateur archaeological society is:

Wisconsin Archeological Society
P.O. Box 1292
Milwaukee, WI 53201

The society has chapters in Madison, Kenosha, and Stevens Point. Membership is $5.50 per year and members receive a quarterly journal, *The Wisconsin Archeologist.*

The Society was organized in 1901. "Its members engage in surface hunting for prehistoric Indian artifacts. Unusual artifacts and other discoveries resulting from such work are often published in the *Archeologist.* A very large part of the surveying and mapping of Indian earthworks, occupation sites and other surface features in the state is accomplished by the non-professionals of the society and is also published in the society's journal. The society conducts archaeological excavations during which members have an opportunity to participate in digs with professional guidance.

"One of the most important functions of the society is to work to preserve the Indian antiquities of the state, and particularly to discourage digging into prehistoric sites through which important scientific information will be lost."

Milwaukee Public Museum
800 West Wells Street
Milwaukee, WI 53233

Wyoming

The state archaeologist for Wyoming is:

Dr. George Frison
Department of Anthropology
University of Wyoming
Arts & Sciences Building
Laramie, WY 82070

The Wyoming Archaeological Society may be reached through the same address.

There are many volumes of materials on archaeological activities in Wyoming. Information may be obtained from:

Buck Dawson
Director
Wyoming State Museums
Barrett Building
Cheyenne, WY 82002

Puerto Rico

Museum of Anthropology
University of Puerto Rico
Rio Pedras, PR

National Organizations

Society for American Archeology
1703 New Hampshire Avenue, N.W.
Washington, D.C. 20009

Index